Mansfield in World War II

Memories from the

People of Mansfield

Published by

The Old Mansfield Society

(c) Old Mansfield Society 2003   ISBN 0-9517948-7-6
Reprinted March 2004
www.old-mansfield.org.uk

Compiled by the following Old Mansfield Members.
                          J. Vanags, (DTP)   P. A. Ashton, (Editor)
M. J. Jackson, T. Gamble, D. Crute, D. Morley, B. Gallon, J. Bretton, M. Eames.

BOOK PRODUCTION WAR ECONOMY STANDARD

THIS BOOK IS PRODUCED IN COMPLETE CONFORMITY WITH THE AUTHORIZED ECONOMY STANDARDS

Printed in England by Technical Print Services Limited, Nottingham.

CONTENTS

Introduction	M. J. Jackson	5
Random Memories	J. A, Taylor	9
Industry in Mansfield	D. Morley	10
Snippets of Industrial Memories		11
The Bevin Boy	A. D. Clay	11
Mansfield at War	R. Cope	16
Recollections	A. D. Clay	18
Rationing	B. Gallon	19
Memories of a Schoolgirl	T. R. Beaumont	20
Education During the War.	H. M. Sutton	22
Memories of Wartime	H. Fisher	22
Family Recollections	D. Kuban	24
Evacuee Who Became my Wife	D.E & L.E Clarke	33
Law and Order	T Gamble	33
My Memories of the War	Mrs Shore	34
My Diary of the War Years	R Sale	35
War Time Reminiscences	J Pollard	38
War Time Memories	B. Renshaw	39
My Wartime Memories	Ms Wragge	43
Remembering The War	S. Bullick	44
An Evacuee from Worthing	Paul Tee	47
Two Memories Kept Secret	J. L. Noble	51
My War Years	Russ Yeamons	51
A Soldier's View of Mansfield.	W. H. Jackson	53
Snippets of Memories		54
Time Line	T. Gamble	58

Other contributors:
    Mrs. Fearn.   Mrs. Gent.   L. Orton.
    Mrs. Wright.   Mr. Smith.   Mr. Hall
    Mrs Shore.   J. A. Taylor.   D Binch
    The Elizabethan - 1944
    Mansfield Advertiser

Mayor's Personal Message

MY DEAR FELLOW CITIZENS,

As your Mayor, I am delighted to share in this " Peace Souvenir." On two occasions it has been my privilege to lead your " Peace and Victory Celebrations." This has been the crowning experience of my year of office. By God's grace we have emerged from a long, dark night of war, and now we stand on the threshold of a new era in the history of mankind. We shall not forget the tremendous sacrifices by which Victory was won. We shall never cease to honour those who fought and died, to preserve our liberties. May God help us to be worthy of these gallant souls.

And now, what of the future? Already there is evidence of difficulties which we must face unitedly. A new Government is faced by colossal tasks, and merits our sympathetic and prayerful support. A magnificent programme of social improvements is going to be enacted. We must regard nothing as impossible, if we approach our new tasks in the right spirit. As Christian people, we believe that God, Who has been our Helper in days of war, will not withhold His help in the difficult days ahead. Let us consecrate ourselves to the task of seeking the best, not for England alone, but for all mankind. Above all, let us accept the leadership of Christ our Saviour. May the Divine Blessing rest upon our Borough, and upon all its Citizens, in the new and challenging period on which we have entered.

Yours most faithfully,

CALEB BROWN,

Mayor.

1945 "Peace and Victory Celebration" message from the Mayor.
Front cover of Peace Day Programme on page 49.

Introduction
Michael Jackson.

The summer of 1939 was a good one. Many local families enjoyed basking in their favourite east coast resorts while Nottinghamshire batsman, Walter Keeton, who lived in Mansfield, had responded to the sun on his back by making the highest score for the county, 312 not out.

People could be forgiven for thinking that just as good, if not better, days lay ahead for had not the Prime Minister, Mr. Neville Chamberlain, assured the nation of, 'Peace in our time.'

Not every one was deceived by such bland promises. Nazi Germany's occupation of the Rhineland, Austria and Czechoslovakia sounded alarm bells that were not altogether unheard. Each war brings its own horror and from the Great War came the fear of poison gas and from the Spanish Civil War the devastation that could be brought about by air raids. Thus, while many enjoyed the sunshine and looked on the bright side, from 1937 volunteers had been enrolled into various civil defence units. Air raid wardens were trained in general duties, first aid and anti-gas measures and equipped with whistles, hand bells and rattles to give warning of different dangers that might arise. Meanwhile, throughout the land people were fitted and issued with gasmasks. These, in their cardboard boxes, hung in the hallways and cupboards: just in case.

Despite earlier assurances of peace, war was declared against Germany on Sunday, the 3rd of September, 1939 following that country's invasion of Poland on the 1st of the month. Hardly had the prime minister finished addressing the nation over the wireless than air raid sirens wailed over the land. Fortunately it was a false alarm but it was a foretaste of a sound that was to bring fear and dread during the next five years. An immediate task in every home was to ensure that all windows were blacked out during the hours of darkness. Such measures varied from elaborate blinds, special curtains and light proof screens to emergency measures such as a blanket tacked into place with drawing pins.

Within two days of the outbreak of the war, previously made plans to evacuate children from what were regarded as prime bombing targets to places of safety were put into effect. Thus, on the 5th of September, Nottingham City buses brought pupils from High Pavement and other schools to Mansfield. The need to find suitable homes for the children and to arrange school accommodation made it necessary to postpone the beginning of the autumn term until later in the month. Some boys, perhaps at a loose end, in the longer holiday, gathered outside the drill hall in Bath Street to watch the Sherwood Rangers who were billeted there, mount and change guard and salute the officers as they entered and left the building. As with all territorial units, local men in the Sherwood Rangers and Sherwood Foresters were immediately mobilised, being transformed from 'Saturday Night Soldiers' to full time fighting men in a matter of hours.

After this initial flurry of activities, Mansfield seemed little affected by the war. True school days were shorter where premises had to be shared with the evacuees, gas masks were supposed to be carried on all occasions and there were empty chairs at the meal time table in many homes but the sirens remained silent, rationing and food shortages were still in the future and the local newspapers contained few, if any, news of casualties. In fact, as the evenings drew in, the only major nuisance was the blackout. With all the windows screened and street lamps and vehicle head lights masked to give the merest slits of light, being out at night was quite hazardous. Bumps were frequent, tumbles quite common and road accidents regular occurrences. Attempts to cope with the blacked out streets led to one of the first shortages of the war. Torches were a vital help in negotiating the sepulchral darkness and soon batteries for the most popular size, No 8, were in short supply. News of their availability in any shop led to a rush of customers to its door and its meagre supply was soon sold out. Memory doesn't recall whether anybody actually queued for No 8 batteries but before long a line of patient shoppers, hopeful of buying some wanted commodity, usually food, was one of the unforgettable sights of the home front.

Despite earlier fears and although some air raid shelters, both public and private, had been made, the air raid siren was silent in blacked out Mansfield. Even so, many people preferred to stay at home at nights rather than risk the difficulties of the unlit streets. Within four walls, the wireless set, not yet known as the radio - assumed a hitherto unknown importance both as a source of news and of entertainment. Newsreaders such as Alvar Lidell attained an almost celebrity status while everyday conversation was peppered with catch phrases from popular variety shows. Of these, although it was not broadcast until later in the war, 'It's That Man Again' - ITMA for short, - featuring Tommy Handley was, perhaps, the greatest favourite and is still fondly remembered today.

In those early months of the war, unless a family had a loved one away in the forces, events touched Mansfield lightly. There were petty nuisances to be borne but the earlier fears of air raids and gas attacks proved groundless. So lacking in danger did the general situation seem that by Christmas of 1939, the children, evacuated in haste in September, had returned home.

This period of inactivity - the 'Phoney War', as it was called - lasted until the early summer of 1940. In this period of comparative calm, there were reminders that, in the popular phrase, 'there's a war on.' Early in January, food rationing was introduced: not all at once, just for meat to begin with but other foods followed. This ensured that every one received a fair share of basic items even if it was a very small one and many Mansfield housewives developed considerable skill in eking out their meagre supplies. Vegetables were more freely available and people were encouraged to grow their own. 'Dig for Victory,' they were urged as lawns, gardens and parks were put to the spade. Allotments flourished. Hitherto unsuspected benefits were attributed to whichever vegetable was in season. Carrots, so it was said, helped night-time vision; of help to those who braved the blackout.

Local men in the forces were not forgotten. In January, the Mayor, Councillor Percy Stafford, launched a fund to provide comforts for over a thousand men who were away from home. Some provision was also made for servicemen stationed in or around Mansfield. Canteens were set up, mainly by churches and chapels and while these served a purpose and were appreciated, the cinemas, dance halls and public houses proved a greater attraction.

The comparative calm of the 'phoney' war came to a sudden and violent end in April 1940, with the German invasion of Denmark and Norway. Although the fighting was many miles away, Mansfield felt very much involved in the conflict, as one of the regiments in the hastily formed expeditionary force that was sent to Norway was the local territorial battalion of the Sherwood Foresters. Outnumbered and ill equipped, some fell in battle, many were taken prisoners: only a few returned safely to England. As they looked at the ever increasing casualty lists in the local papers no Mansfield person could be in any doubt that they and their home town were now fully involved in the war and must face its consequences. One of these was the return of the evacuees; this time from Southend when over eight hundred children were billeted in the town and shared school accommodation with local children. Most of them remained until 1944, many forging life long friendships. A more poignant sight was that of battle weary soldiers sent to the town to recuperate after surviving the dangers of the Dunkirk evacuation.

For some months, with the army under strength and the enemy twenty or so miles away across the English Channel, invasion was an imminent threat. To help combat this, a new civilian force was formed, chiefly of men too old for the forces or in reserved occupations. Originally known as the Local Defence Volunteers, they were later called the Home Guard though now, following the gently mocking television series, they are remembered as 'Dad's Army.' Mansfield's men folk, by the hundred, flocked to join this new force. They drilled, marched, mounted guard, fired their rifles and, doubtless, duties for the day over, reminisced of their time on the Western Front more than twenty years earlier.

An opening phase of the war came to its sudden and violent end and the fate of the nation lay in the balance, Mansfield braced itself for whatever efforts were demanded of it. Apart from the passage of an occasional stray enemy aircraft, it was spared the horrors of air raids though it heard the sound of exploding bombs when Nottingham was attacked and saw the red glow in the northern sky when Sheffield was blitzed. However it tightened its belt to cope with the full rigours of food rationing, it saw its factories and workshops turn to the production of the necessities of war, its young people called to the colours and many of those remaining directed to war work. Its people bought a Spitfire, contributed to National Savings campaigns, gave their saucepans to help aircraft production and saw their garden railings go for similar purposes. It was a hard time, a worrying time for those with loved ones in the forces but it was also a time of determination to face all the difficulties that arose until final victory was eventually achieved.

Territorials, outside Evinsons Garage, 1938. Training with the prospect of an approaching war.

A 'Back Your Boys' procession in support of National Savings, 21st. June 1941.

Random memories
J A Taylor

I was 5 when the war started. And I had just begun my schooling at Moor Lane Infants. I suppose it would be in 1940 that a school from Essex was evacuated to Mansfield, and we went on a 'shift' system with them. Mornings one week, afternoons the next. I cannot remember how long this went on, but do remember that my individually named coat-peg suddenly also became the facility of one Bobby Abbott. I think later the classes must have been integrated because I kept in touch with one 'Essex boy', Richard King, for quite a time afterwards.

As children one thing we did was to chalk a Nazi swastika on our hands and them thump people on the back, leaving the chalk impression. Very funny!

We lived at No 1 Brick Kiln Lane and my parents made a tremendous contribution to the war effort that has never been fully recognised. Every night, week after week, whatever the weather, they would collect Rueben Hopkinson from the farm next door (in the V of Brick Kiln Lane and Skegby Lane - now demolished) and they would walk (no petrol) the 50 yards to 'The Sir John Cockle'. There, with no thought for their own safety, they would sit in the Lounge Bar night after night, sometimes, when beer was short, with little to drink, looking towards Sutton for German panzer tanks. They were quite dedicated to this. Family folk law suggests that Adolf Hitler got to know of this duty, realised it would be hopeless to invade Mansfield from the South West, and so never did.

At what is now the crossroads at the 'Cockle' were large concrete barriers, with 'portable' concrete pillars that could have been inserted, theoretically, to block the road and prevent a German advance.

On Garnon Street, just off Brick Kiln Lane, an air raid shelter was built taking up half the road. So far

Plaque at the Kings Mill U.S. Army Hospital.

as I know it was never used in anger, but as children we used it for 'hide and seek' games.

The American army built what is now King's Mill Hospital on its present site. I think local residents must have been encouraged to offer hospitality, because we often entertained Doctors and Nurses of the American Army. Indeed one specialist, Major Alan Palmer, became the godfather of my sister Susan (now Wilson) and she went to stay with him and his family in San Francisco many years later.

Similarly, my Grandfather lived at Kings Mill House (now demolished), a farm at the Mansfield end of the reservoir. There a front room was put aside for American Officers to use as a small 'mess'. (Perhaps the fact that they seemed to have unlimited supplies of whisky was a factor!). At any rate it was used extensively and again family folklore has it that Clarke Gable attended when attached to the hospital.

German prisoners of war were sent to work on farms, one 'Herman' to King's Mill. My late uncle Jim, who was in the Royal Signals, grew friendly with Herman, and often, when on leave, would lend Herman his uniform to wear while both of them walked along to 'The Cockle' for a drink!

On the Mansfield side of the hospital was an Italian Prisoner of War Camp. I can remember the barbed

Clarke Gable at the Kings Mill US Army Hospital.

wire fencing all round - although never heard of any escape attempt. The prisoners were employed to dig trenches around the neighbourhood, I suppose for the Home Guard etc to use in case of any invasion.

The 'Air Raid Warning' and 'All Clear' sirens were often heard. I think they were on top of Moor Lane School.

German aeroplanes were also often heard, but Sheffield or Nottingham appeared to be their targets. I do not think any bombs dropped near Mansfield. British fighter planes, Hurricanes and Spitfires etc, were always about as were Lancaster and Wellington bombers and we got quite expert in 'spotting' the different makes. Later, as the Americans became involved, Flying Fortresses were very common.

Savings were encouraged at school. One year a Spitfire was brought to Mansfield market place and schoolchildren encouraged to come and see it, sit in the seat, and meet the Mayor.

Life was, of course, different. There were not many cars about and petrol was rationed. Journeys had to be justified. When my sister was born my father was stopped one night taking the (youngish, rather attractive) midwife home. He had some difficulty in establishing his reasons!

I suppose, as young children in Mansfield, during the war we were not affected very much. Food and clothing were rationed, but my mother seemed to cope and we never starved, although of course there was nothing like the variety of food now available. There were no sweets or bananas etc. but never really having had them we did not miss them.

The actual war was very distant and, with no TV, not very immediate. We took the planes, soldiers and tanks etc. much for granted. Thankfully my own family suffered no tragedies and all relations returned home safely.

Industry During the War
D. Morley

The war had a number of effects upon the industry of the area. In mining the main object was to maximise output. Very little development was carried out the major development was the introduction of the Meco-Moore cutter-loader which improved production. Otherwise there was little change so that by the end of hostilities mines were rather antiquated. William Hollins & Co, Pleasley Vale were in a somewhat downturn at the beginning of the war and things got much better, war contracts reviving the situation after the previous hard times.

Mrs D Davies started work at the mills on leaving school in 1941. Her impressions on going through the door for the first time were 'With the war being on we'd blackout and there were no lights in the yard or anything... When we got inside all the electric lights had gone out so it was pitch black. Then the lights came on.' The war contracts meant that the threads produced were either navy blue or khaki. With the new business it was shift work. In those days no overalls were provided. Clothing was rationed and you needed precious coupons to procure it, but, clothing coupons were not needed for blackout curtains, so the workers, made their own overalls using that material. Mrs Davies comments that she

Mansfield escaped serious air raids during the Second World War though people's sleep was often broken by the drone of enemy bombers flying overhead. Perhaps it was the thought of hitting back at them that made the local Spitfire Fund so successful. Once launched, people were encouraged to raise £5,000 which was the cost of one of these aircraft. Mansfield's fund soon reached its target and the Spitfire on the photograph was duly named **Sherwood Forester**. It flew operationally for almost a year before being converted for photographic reconnaissance work. On 19-July 1953, while on a training flight in poor visibility, it crashed into a hillside on the Isle of Skye.

21, 1943.

TARGETS to be ADOPTED.
NEXT WEEK.

Many savings schemes were introduced to help the war effort.

LANCASTER BOMBER PRICE £40,000	MOSQUITO BOMBER PRICE £20,000	SUNDERLAND FOUR-ENGINED FLYING BOAT PRICE £50,000	CATALINA FLYING BOAT PRICE £20,000
is being paid for by MANSFIELD WOODHOUSE SAVINGS' GROUPS.	is being paid for by THE SCHOOLS OF THE MANSFIELD BOROUGH.	is being paid for by The MANSFIELD SAVINGS BANK.	is being paid for by THE STREETS GROUPS OF MANSFIELD.

had a 'dressmaker to make me some overalls, black overalls and bright red bias binding on pockets and sleeves. They looked nice, but when you washed them two or three times they went a horrible grey and all the dye came out'.

When the male workforce began to be called up into the armed forces the women started to take over their jobs. Miss P Fletcher began working at William Hollins on the spinning machines. BSA set up a munitions factory in the Vale and she moved to them. She worked on drilling and tapping machines and also capstan lathes making the firing pin for anti-tank guns. She did this for three years. When the war ended she moved to Whiteley Radio working similar machines and eventually becoming a chargehand.

The war caused shortages of materials at the Mansfield Brewery so when forces personnel came home to Mansfield on leave they were often unable to be given a pint for lack of production.

At Barringer, Wallis and Manners, later to become part of Metal Box, about half of production was turned over to helping the war effort.

Joyce Bryant joined the company in 1942 as a teenager 'doing respirators for gas masks . . . also mess tins . . . and bomb tails. It was shift work, but I was unable to go on nights because I wasn't old enough. You had to be eighteen to go on nights. So, that put me out of nights. I just did days and afternoons.' The morning shift was six am till two pm and the afternoon shift was two till ten pm. Hand presses were used at this time. Power presses came later on. Passes were needed to enter the works gates and you had to carry your gas mask with you for which the firm provided a carrying tin. In addition to the gas masks and mess tins in the early period of the war they were also contracted to make the Boyes Anti-tank Rifle, a one-man weapon which fired an armour-piercing half-inch round. During the invasion scares of 1940 and 1941 they were standard issue for units on anti-invasion duties and for the RAF Regiment. Later on the company made the Very pistol and the Sten machine carbine.

Another aspect of the war effort was the raising of money for War Bonds. The schemes were to raise £5000, the notional cost of a Spitfire aircraft. The Metal Box group set up one of these schemes and all member companies of the group participated. By May 1941 an aircraft had been bought - Spitfire Mk2b serial P8389, carrying the name 'Metabox'. It survived the war, being scrapped in 1947.

James Maude & Co, iron founders, was another company who turned over most of their production into Ministry work in the period 1939 - 1945.

Mr G Edgeson joined Boneham & Turner, precision engineers, in 1938, working for them for 49 years and finishing as technical foreman. Because of the quality of their work, when war started in 1939 they were immediately put on the government list of essential services and got a lot of orders from government departments 'and it was all hell let loose. The factory at Duke Street became a magician's workshop because we'd got all old machinery and we were expected to produce these precision parts for the aircraft industry. They had to be done to strict government limits and all we'd got to do them on was old machines. We couldn't get new machines because the government operated a priority system . . . We were at the bottom of the priority list'. The company produced parts for Bristol Aircraft Corporation, Rolls Royce, De Havilland. During the war there was a community spirit. Mr Edgeson goes on, "During the war you'd come to work in a morning and even though there was a war on you were always allowed about a quarter of an hour to get yourself organised and your machine warmed up . . . During that time you'd form little groups and discuss what was on the radio the night before . . . ITMA (It's That Man Again, Tommy Handley) was the programme that boosted the morale of the country . . . All the jokes were repeated and we had a damn good laugh. Then everybody got stuck in. Mostly they worked from eight am till often nine o'clock in the evening. If the news was bad, such as during the time of Dunkirk, everybody had visions of Germans coming over. It wasn't nice at all . . . It's a job to keep spirits up . . . When the bombers used to come over you could see Sheffield being plastered. During the war employee numbers were about 400. They made the tailfin of the Lancaster bomber. Thousands of jig bushes and dowel pins were made for use in the drilling of rivet holes in aircraft panels by six specially built grinding machines, operated by women, assisted by a pensioner. Also a line of bench lathes were operated by women, one of whom, Mrs Mary Lee, Blidworth Road, Fishpool, was awarded the MBE for her work on these machines. The machines were built by the firm. In addition to aircraft work press tool sets were made for producing parts of Bren guns, milling fixtures for 20mm cannon and even press tool sets to produce sand goggle frames."

The war made many changes to the work place. Women took over in many previously considered male occupations and companies were revived after the depressions of the pre war years.

Snippets of Industrial Memories

D. A. Clay

Birmingham Small Arms took over the ground floor of the Doubling Room of Harwood Cash & Co Ltd, Lawn Mills, Rosemary Street, to manufacture barrels for the Bren Gun. Lawn Mills were processing heavy yarn to be used for webbing, haversacks, water bottle carriers and ammunition pouches, etc. Whiteleys were engaged in manufacturing wireless and parts and radar items.

Boneham & Turners, Nottingham Road factory, made parts for the Lancaster bomber tail assemblies.

M. Hall

Mother worked in Barringers making munitions. The children were put to bed at school in the afternoon, while their mothers were at work.

Sheffield bombing was felt in Mansfield making houses shake.

Mining - The Bevin Boy
Mr. A. D. Clay

The name came from the then Minister of Labour, Ernest Bevin M.P., who started the conscription of men into the pits. In 1944 many men registering for National Service were made to work down the pits instead of going into the armed forces. I was one of those. Even though I had done all my training in the Army Cadets and I was looking forward to going in the army.

On the 4th September 1944 I was sent to the government training centre at Creswell Colliery – to be trained for underground work in the coalmines. On reporting we were issued with a white helmet, blue boilersuit and a pair of pit boots with external metal toecaps, metal heelguards and hobnailed soles – very heavy. All kitted up we were sent on a march round Cresswell and Whitwell with the P.T. instructors. It was a very cold September day and I felt the cold having come from working in the very warm environment of Harwood Cash & Co, Lawn Mills. We were accompanied by the jeers of villagers who thought we were dodging the services.

The next day we went down the pit for the first time and the winders took great delight in dropping us as fast as they could into the bowels of the earth. From here we visited the training face where over the next week we were taught erecting, ripping and coal getting by the old colliers. We were also shown haulage jobs such as 'lockering up' tub wheels, clipping-on and knocking-off clips, lashing tubs to an overhead rope haulage (fingers look out!). When we

MANSFIELD AND MANSFIELD WOODHOUSE

WARSHIP WEEK, 1942.

This Diploma of Merit

IS AWARDED TO

Messrs. D. Pothecary Ltd. Group 159/6/4

WHICH INCREASED ITS AVERAGE WEEKLY SAVINGS OF £9 : 15 S. 0 D.

TEN FOLD

AND RAISED THE SUM OF £125 : 0 S. 0 D.

DURING WARSHIP WEEK.

President.
Frank Hardy, Chairman.
Hon. Secretary.

HMS ICARUS - Adopted by Mansfield, she had a distinguished service record.

(Image from www.warships.com).

came out of the pit we played football with about 50 per team in our new pit boots.

Each night we would thumb a lift into Warsop in our dirty clothing. Once we had a lift in a flour lorry, we came out looking like ghosts! From Warsop we caught the bus to Mansfield and then another as far as Eakring Road to get home.

On finishing our training at Creswell (Mr Inverarity was the manager) we were allocated to other pits. I went to Crown Farm Colliery, Mansfield. At the pit we worked on the pit top for an initial period in a terrible winter of thick snow. After a time we were drafted underground to work in the pit bottom. My first job was 'slinging' at £2.15s.0d. per week, gross. This meant lifting the clips and couplers off the full tubs as they came into the bottom, hooking them on to a rope attached to the wall, sliding them beyond the shaft to the empty side into the empty tubs for transport back to the face loading point.

We had to be down the pit so as to start winding coal at 6.50am and work until 3pm. I progressed from the pit bottom to '7's and '5's district empties clipping on point and sending tubs up to the two panels. Then I went to 'steadying in', where runs of coal came into the bottom (15 tubs at a time) ready for transport up the pit. From here I went up to '4's trunk road accepting runs of coal from '7's and '5's districts. When the cablebelt was installed it was decided to tip Top Hard Coal in the pit bottom onto a short belt (I was operating this tippler for a while) onto the cablebelt and into the mine cars that were pulled by locos to the pit bottom.

After that I went on underground signals and then to the electric staff, progressing from Trainee Electrician to Electrician of the Mine to Assistant Electrical Engineer.

Some Random Memories
Three people to a locker, George Organ, Jock Campbell and myself fighting for clothes and towels in one locker, both clean and dirty side.

The lovely dinners that we had because we were manual workers, who were entitled to over and above the usual rations. It cost one shilling – 10d. for the dinner and 2d. for the sweet - in the canteen under the pithead baths. We also received an extra cheese ration.

The longing to get rid of the white helmet and wear a black helmet like the ordinary miners who looked down on the Bevin Boys.

Being issued with food packs meant for the forces in the Far East. There were chocolates, cigarettes, tins of fruit and other goodies. This was 1946/47.

1946/47 Wintertime shortages of railway wagons, which meant paid days off until more arrived. These holidays were called 'Bevins', paid under E.W.O. (Essential Work Orders).

A Bevin Boy Hostel on Clipstone Road, Forest Town. Later it was used as the Police Training Centre and later as a hostel for refugees from Eastern Europe. Some Bevin Boys were in private digs instead of living at the hostel.

Each Friday, pay was presented in a small tin can from which you had to fight to get the paper money out.

There were a lot of ponies in the pit. They were very clever, they would not pull more than their allotted number of tubs despite the efforts or brutality of the pony drivers. The ponies lived in stables underground, which were kept well whitewashed and well lit. The ponies came up periodically for a rest in the pony field next to Eakring Road. They were brought up the pit on a Saturday morning and taken to the field gate where they were set free. They went mad, kicking up their hooves and loving the freedom.

10th June 1940

'The Military are still in occupation of the schools. Half of the pupils are at Nottingham Road Methodist Schoolroom on Gedling Street, and half on Forest Road, alternating mornings and afternoons'.

24th June 1940

'The top four classes are housed in High Oakham School, the four junior classes remaining in the Nottingham Road Schoolroom. Life was much easier at High Oakham, in a purpose built school.

12th July 1940

School closed for a week.

22nd July 1940

'King Edward's reopens and, as High Oakham School is on holiday, all classes are held there'.

29th July 1940

'Back at King Edward's again! Everything looks exactly as it was left, exercise books and needlework still in the cupboards'

'I'm sure we found it rather dull having to work normally for the short time before the school year ended. At least there were no exams or reports!'

Carter Lane Junior School

Carter Lane Junior School was also closed for the same reason and where the children went I do not know.

However, I can remember my mother who was in the Red Cross going up to help. She saw a soldier writing a letter to his family to say he was safe. She offered to post it. He shouted to the rest of the soldiers that they were to give their letter to her and that she would post them. She ended up with a big pile and our local dairyman, when he delivered our milk that teatime, seeing the pile on the kitchen table ready for posting offered to pay the postage.

Recollections
A. D. Clay

The survivors of the British Expeditionary Force from Dunkirk arrived at the LNER station on Great Central Road. They were haggard, unshaven, half without arms, boots, tunics or any other equipment, they nevertheless formed up and marched through the town and up to the Market Place from where they were split up and were allocated billets. Some of the billets used were the Palais de Danse, Leeming Street; the Drill Hall, Bath Street; Henley Hall, Portland Street; Queens Hall, Belvedere Street; several schools; and the Town Hall, where some soldiers came out onto the balcony and threw foreign coins to the children waiting below

Sometime after Dunkirk some American soldiers were calling a group of Dunkirk veterans 'Dunkirk Harriers' who did not take kindly to their remarks and so they despatched one Yank through a plate glass window opposite the Victoria Hotel, Albert Street.

Mr. Hibbert at 1 Montague Street.

Rationing
Barbara Gallon

Rationing was introduced in January 1940, initially for butter, sugar, bacon and ham. Housewives, who remembered the shortage of food in the Great War, had already stocked up with sugar and dry goods, also preserved fresh eggs in crocks of isinglass, although these were unpalatable when boiled, but were edible when scrambled.

A National Loaf made of wholewheat flour, noted for its greyish colour and firm texture, could be freshened up by soaking in cold water and re-baking. Throughout the war years, a campaign to eat more potatoes instead of bread resulted in a proliferation of recipes for that vegetable. Garden owners were urged to 'Dig for Victory' and former flower beds in Carr Bank and Titchfield Park were used as allotments, although park attendants needed to keep a sharp eye on boys who persistently stole produce or stamped on plants.

The lease-lend agreement with the U.S.A. began on the 31st of May 1941, and importation of Orange Juice for children, Dried Eggs in tins or packets and the much relished and versatile tinned Spam were welcomed. The first American G. I,'s landed in January 1942, bearing gifts of coveted nylon stockings and chewing gum.

The Ministry of Food initiated a weekday Kitchen Front Broadcast on the Home service wireless programme at 8.15am, giving helpful hints and recipes. A regular feature in national and local newspapers titled 'Food Facts' gave recipes, methods of dealing with foodstuffs, some quite alien to British housewives such as Soya flour, whale meat and dogfish and complete menus for a week or more. The Minister of Food, Lord Woolton gave his name to a vegetable pie covered with potato pastry.

In canteens and restaurants, customers were urged to select dishes from the menu marked with a V, indicating that these were 'ship savers' with no imported ingredients. After July 1940 it was illegal to serve a customer with more than one main dish at any restaurant meal.

Mansfield's British Restaurant opened in Belvedere Street on 15th May 1941, with accommodation for 240 diners. For 11d, a customer had soup, bread, meat, vegetables, a sweet and a cup of tea. A child's meal cost 6d. With the three cookery centres in school canteens already operating, Mansfield people unable to return home for dinner, were well catered for. Altogether, up to 1,000 midday meals were served each weekday.

Many pantries in the town testified to the skills of those women who processed fruit and vegetables in times of plenty, compensating for scarcity of tinned fruit. Bottled plums and gooseberries, (without sugar), jams, sauces and chutneys provided welcome variations to an often monotonous diet. Young runner beans could be salted but needed to be soaked for two hours before cooking.

An Adult Ration for One Week in 1942.

Bacon, ham, meat - 4ozs (100gr) - 1s 2d (6p).
Butter - 2ozs (50gr).
Cheese - 2ozs (50gr) sometimes 4ozs.
Cooking Fat - 4ozs (100gr) reduced to 2ozs at times.
Milk - 3 pints but reduced to 2 at times. Skimmed or dried milk available.
Sugar - 8ozs (225gr).
Preserves - 1lb every 2 months.
Tea - 2ozs (50gr).

Eggs - 1 shell egg a week if available.
Dried eggs - 1 packet in 4 weeks.
Sweets - 12 ozs (350gr) every 4 weeks.

Memoirs of a Schoolgirl
T.R. Beaumont

I was 10 years old and starting the Queen Elizabeth's Girls Grammar School. My sister was just 4 years old. As far as bombing went we didn't really know much about that.

We had to have blackout curtaining as well as our own curtains and the warden would knock at the door if you were showing a light. We had shutters up at the bathroom and lavatory windows with teddy bears on them. The windows were crisscrossed with special tape so the glass wouldn't fly about if broken.

[Ed.: After the first practice on 27 Jan. 1939 the blackout was imposed for real on 1 Sept. and rigorously enforced. Breaches of the regulations were so numerous, e.g. 40 at one Court sitting in October, that evening sessions were held to deal with them and high numbers of offences continued right up March 1945 when the regulations were partially relaxed before being ended in April]

Food was rationed and it was hard to get good meals. We were lucky we had market gardeners who had stalls on the market and we could get fresh vegetables. A lot of people grew their own vegetables. Imported fruit was also non-existent. We had some fruit bushes, gooseberries, raspberries, black and red currants.

[Ration books were issued in November 1939 for rationing to begin in December for bacon, ham (4 ounces per week) and butter (2 ounces), followed within a few weeks by other basic foodstuffs. Unrationed items, especially tinned goods, became scarce and rocketed in price. Customers and shopkeepers found the complicated rationing regulations irksome and inevitably sought ways round them.]

Food was rationed and you had to make everything last, so housewives thought up things to do. My mum mixed the 'marge' and butter together which made the 'marge' taste better. You saved bacon fat and mixed it with the lard for pastry. We got dried egg in the rations and I loved omelettes made with it, keep thinking I will try it again.

We kept hens and one cockerel. Dad built a lovely hen house on wheels so he could move it round the garden - we had a long garden - there was also a run but they spent a lot of time free to roam. I loved going and getting the eggs out of the nest-boxes. Mum also raised chicks to replace the old hens when they were laying no longer. One broody hen would raise a good family and the hens would give us extra meat. Mum also put down eggs in a large earthenware crock with a wooden lid and preserved them with isinglass (It was Sodium Silicate and, mixed with an equal amount of water, prevented the air, which would turn the eggs bad, seeping through the pores of the shells) so we had eggs when the hens were not laying.

We had to share our school for a time. We each went for half a day and every other Saturday.

[After a delayed start to the new school year the Girls Grammar School hosted pupils from the Manning School in Nottingham until the end of the Autumn term 1939 when those evacuees returned home. Other schools in Mansfield had a similar experience because of the many hundreds of children, mothers and expectant mothers billeted in the Mansfield area from Nottingham, Sheffield, Southend, Scotland and, later. Greater London. Some returned home fairly quickly, but in April 1945 there were 941 official plus 1,963 unofficial evacuees (some without homes to return to) still in Mansfield]

The siren was on top of our Junior School on Carter Lane. After Dunkirk it housed soldiers who were suffering from shell-shock and were very tired. Locals were asked to take one or two for Sunday dinner when we could. They gave us extra rations for this. We always had a couple.

My Dad built a beautiful shelter in the garden for us. It must have been 7ft. deep, 10ft. long to allow for steps up and 6ft. wide. There were 4 bunk beds and steps up with a trap to pull down. It was covered with soil and grass. It was very cosy indeed. We saw very little bombing so in the end we stopped using it. If the sirens went my parents turned the settee on its front against an inside wall and my sister and I slept under that.

[Not every household had its own shelter, the Town Council having decided in September 1939 not to distribute Anderson shelters, but it did issue advice about preparing a 'refuge room' in the house. The Council sought to provide public shelters by having trenches dug at Carr Bank, Clumber St., Queen St., Bath Lane and Titchfield Park. It also surveyed caves and cellars in the town centre, a list of which was published on 15 September 1939. The start of the new school term was delayed to allow shelters to be built and by 6 October 1939, with 7 new shelters under construction. All schools were provided for except Rosemary St., which apparently did not have a suitable space.]

Most things had to be queued for and sometimes the shop ran out before you got inside. Once a week we went to what was called the British Restaurant on Belvedere St. for a dinner. I cannot remember what they charged but it would be very little.

[The British Restaurant was ceremonially opened by the Mayor, Councillor. H. Baggaley, at the old Picturedrome in Belvedere St. on 15 May 1941. It offered the same menu every day at the following prices, soup 1d; meat course with vegetables 6d; sweet 2d; tea 1d. per cup.]

Coal was limited and we put the slack dust into sugar bags, wet it and let it dry and used them.

Nothing was wasted. Sticks for the fire were not very plentiful, so we took the sheets of the big newspaper, rolled them up tight and then plaited them together. They worked very well.

Mum and a circle of her friends met together once a week in each other's houses. They had adopted a Merchant Navy ship and knitted seaboot stockings and sweaters in oiled wool for the men. They also knitted 6inch squares in any wool they could get from people and sewed them together for blankets. That was how I learned to knit.

[Ed. In January 1940 the Mayor opened a fund to supply comforts for servicemen, particularly such things as gloves, scarves and socks. Various bodies responded by forming knitting circles and the WVS set up a collection centre at Brunt's Trustees Building in Bath Lane.]

Utility Clothes came in during the war, but you had to have coupons to buy anything in the clothes or bedding line. I'm sure it must have been very hard for some people.

The Utility mark introduced in 1941.

[Clothes rationing began in June 1941 and may have accounted for a sharp rise in the rate of shoplifting at Marks & Spencers and BHS, especially for such things as stockings and underwear. Most of the restrictions on austerity clothing were removed by 1946 but the Utility scheme continued on other goods in a less strict form until 1952.]

We were lucky in Mansfield really as we knew very

little about the bombing. We did some Christmas shopping in Sheffield one year and when we got home there were two bagatelle boards in the box and we had paid for only one. When we took it back the next week there was no shop, Sheffield had been very badly bombed during the week. Some people in Mansfield could see the fires in the distance.

Education during the War
Based on notes by **H.M. Sutton** of the Art College

The declaration of war brought about a closure of all evening classes. Staff and students gradually drifted away to join H. M. Forces and essential war service occupations. Machine tools and lathes were removed from the Technical College for use in factories and, inevitably, shortages of all art and craft materials created difficulties.

After the arrival of the Southend - on - Sea evacuees in June 1940, the County Director of Education met the principals of the Art School and the Technical College, Mr. H. M. Sutton and Mr. L. Orange, and the Head of Southend College to arrange further education of all students. Ultimately, the decision to merge them into a corporate body with a common timetable was decided, rather than to introduce a system of shift working. Teething troubles surfaced at an early stage. Many of the Southend Staff were over age for National Service and, due to depletion by 'call up', of experienced younger Mansfield tutors, their places were filled by temporary appointments. The Southend Principal promptly joined the forces and it was left to Mr Sutton to carry the not inconsiderable burden of uniting a disparate body of staff to ensure the smooth running of the curriculum.

A limited number of evening classes in popular subjects were resumed.

Staff and students mounted exhibitions in the town and produced publicity materials for organizations such as Civil Defence, War Savings and Nursing groups. Tutors gave lectures in the Museum, helping to maintain optimism during this dark time.

New demands were made upon the school as members of H.M. Forces stationed in the area attended evening courses for various periods, to be followed by American G. I.'s (with more fanciful ideas), then by German and Italian P.O.W.'s from Cuckney and Sutton Road Camps and, finally, refugees from Europe.

At the end of the war ex - service personnel sought courses in preparation for a return to civilian life. The machines and tools requisitioned in 1939 were finally returned in March 1946.

Memories of Wartime
H Fisher

As I wasn't born until early 1935, my earliest memory is of hearing my Father and elder brothers talking of impending war and preparing for it. I recall my Father hanging on to every news bulletin on the wireless usually read by Alvar Lidell. Our old wireless had an earth wire trapped in the metal window frame and buried in the ground. It was my job to, occasionally, pour a bowl of water onto this wire, in order to stop the crackling noise, which interrupted the broadcasts.

The effects of the war soon became apparent, with the 'blackout'. If one chink of light was seen coming from your house, you soon had the Air Raid Warden hammering on your door and telling you in no uncertain terms to cover it. My Father was in the A.R.P. and had a hooded carbide lamp on his pushbike. Later on we were to hear the drone of German planes heading (as my Father informed us) for Sheffield and Coventry.

It wasn't long before my two eldest brothers were

A.F.W 4026.

Certificate of Proficiency
HOME GUARD

On arrival at the Training Establishment, Primary Training Centre or Recruit Training Centre, the holder must produce this Certificate at once for the officer commanding, together with Certificate A if gained in the Junior Training Corps or Army Cadet Force.

PART I. I hereby certify that (Rank) Sgt. (Name and initials) SMITH E. of H.Q. ~~Battery~~ Company 6th Notts. ~~Regiment~~ Battalion HOME GUARD has qualified in the Proficiency Badge tests as laid down in the pamphlet "Qualifications for, and Conditions governing the Award of the Home Guard Proficiency Badges and Certificates" for the following subjects :—

Subject	Date	Initials
1. General knowledge (all candidates)	22.5.44	A Tuplin LT
2. Rifle	2.4.44	H Pyn L.T.
3. ~~36 M Grenade~~		
*4. (a) ~~Other weapon~~		
(b) ~~Signalling~~		
*5. (a) ~~Battlecraft,~~ (b) ~~Coast Artillery,~~ (c) ~~Heavy A.A. Bty. work,~~ (d) ~~"Z" A.A. Battery work,~~ (e) ~~Bomb Disposal,~~ (f) ~~Watermanship,~~ (g) M.T.	3 May 44	John Hodgson
*6. (a) Map Reading, (b) ~~Field works,~~ (c) ~~First Aid~~	22.5.44	T. Spedding Lt

Date 2 Apr. 1944   Signature T. Marlin maj.
                                 * President or Member of the Board.

Date 22 MAY 1944   Signature T. Marlin maj.
                                 * President or Member of the Board.

Date .... 194...   Signature ....
                                 * President or Member of the Board.

Date .... 194...   Signature ....
                                 * President or Member of the Board.

Date .... 194...   Signature ....
                                 * President or Member of the Board.

PART II. I certify that (Rank) Sgt. (Name and initials) SMITH E. of H.Q. ~~Battery~~ Company 6th Notts. ~~Regiment~~ Battalion HOME GUARD, having duly passed the Proficiency tests in the subjects detailed above in accordance with the pamphlet and is hereby authorized to wear the Proficiency Badge as laid down in Regulations for the Home Guard, Vol. 1, 1942, para. 41d.

Date MAY 26 1944 194...   Signature H.N. Mee Lt.Colonel.
                           Commanding 6th Notts H.G.

PART III. If the holder joins H.M. Forces, his Company or equivalent Commander will record below any particulars which he considers useful in assessing the man's value on arrival at the T.E., P.T.C., R.T.C., e.g. service, rank, duties on which employed, power of leadership, etc.

Date .... 194...   Signature ....
* Delete where not applicable.   O.C.

called up for the forces, one to the Fleet Air Arm and one in the Army. For one so young, this took some getting used to, not having them around, as I was the youngest of four boys and five girls. (Yes, families were usually big in those days). My sister Rosa also went into the A.T.S. which depleted the family even further.

Among the initial turmoil of war, families had to pull together. My sister, Jean, who was older by two years, and I found ourselves doing numerous tasks about the house. Such as feeding Dad's poultry on the back yard and fetching the eggs then cleaning the pen out. Shopping being the main job as we were still a big family. As Mam used to bake her own bread, I used to go to Mrs. Roger's shop on Bright Square at Bull Farm for two pennyworth of balm (yeast) but by the time I got home, there was only one penn'orth as I had eaten the rest. I never knew if Mam noticed, but she never said anything. I used to dread washday, as my job was to turn the mangle whilst Mam fed the washing between the big heavy wooden rollers, at the same time tightening them down with two 't' shaped handles on top. The kitchen was like an oven as it also housed the old copper where Mam boiled the clothes.

It wasn't long before we were issued with gas masks, which had to be carried everywhere, including school, and woe betide you if you were seen without it. Luckily we never had to wear them for any length of time, which was a blessing as they were horrendous things.

Then came the air raid shelters. These sprang up like mushrooms as if by magic. I don't know if the staff were breaking any rules, but the shelter at Bull Farm Junior School was used for keeping gardening equipment in. At Gardening Lessons we would go in and change into old wooden clogs and bring out the spades and rakes etc.

It was one of the air raid shelters situated at the junction of Ruskin Road and Abbott Road at Bull Farm, which earned me the only physical pain from my Dad's belt. Mam had been down town one Saturday and bought me a new pair of short grey trousers, which were meant for going to school in. As the shelter was built into sandstone and as it sloped it made a wonderful slide, but not in the new trousers!! Hence the one and only time my Dad warmed my backside.

Eventually, along came rationing. Whilst clothing and food took priority with adults, us children were more interested in sweet coupons which allowed you one and a quarter pounds of sweets per month. This however did not raise too much of a problem as there was either no sweets to be had or you had no money, with Dad being the only breadwinner (no family allowances in those days) food rightly took priority. School meals must have been a godsend for most parents even though they were very basic. For my own part I came to detest mashed 'tater' and turnip. We would be served this about three times a week at school and get the same for tea at home!! Sago and semolina came into the same category. Dried egg was one of my favourites, with Mam's homemade bread and butter.

And so life went on for 6 long years, the struggle for survival, making your own entertainment (listening to a crackling wireless) and, I suppose, counting your blessings. There are thousands who never got the chance. Hence the futility of war!

Family Recollections
Doris Kuban

I was a young bride of five weeks when war with Germany was declared on 3rd September, 1939. I was living in temporary accommodation on Linden Road, Forest Town before moving to a rented house on Heather Way, Mansfield. The majority of working class people at that time lived in similar rented property

Prior to my marriage I was a stocking 'heeler' at Mansfield Hosiery Mills, being one of the first girls to be employed when the firm opened. The factory entrance was on Harrington Street and not the Botany Avenue entrance as remembered by most people today.

I left my job after marrying to become a full-time housewife, as this was the normal custom at the time. My husband, Douglas Bailey was a hosiery knitter working at Seal and Turner's factory on Kirkland Avenue, and I remember him having to go there to help set up the 'blackouts' on the Sunday war was declared. He remained working as a hosiery knitter until receiving his call-up papers in 1940, when he volunteered for service in the Royal Navy. He remained in the navy from 17th June, 1940 until 21st January, 1946 when he was released after serving on minesweepers throughout the war, and after its conclusion when mines had to be cleared from the sea lanes around Hamburg, Cuxhaven and Ostend.

I had only been married a few months when I contracted rheumatic fever, but even though very ill I refused to go into Victoria Hospital as this did not have a very good reputation at that time (possibly due to its past connections with the workhouse).

There was no National Health Service then, and I was very fortunate that my doctor was extremely caring and visited me every day and night when required. He also had to supply all the necessary medication, as this was not available through a dispensing chemist as would be expected today.

My husband still had to go to work of course, and my father and mother, Fred and Nellie Mills, used to take it in turns with my sister-in-law, Gladys Groves, to stop with me to ensure that I was never alone. I was most grateful to them and my neighbours at that time.

I was still not fully recovered from rheumatic fever when Doug had to start his naval training at HMS Ganges, near Chatham, Kent, and it was thought advisable that I moved in with my parents and younger brother, Fred (known as 'Sonny' to distinguish him from his father) at 77, Layton Avenue. I ended up staying with them for the remainder of the war.

I was allowed to make two visits, each being of one week's duration to see Doug at his training establishment in Sheerness. I travelled to London by train, continuing on by the underground system and then train again to Sheerness. I got a drink of tea at a Salvation Army kiosk at a tube station and remember seeing where the local people used the station as an air raid shelter.

The visits to Sheerness were particularly memorable as the area was bombed whilst I was there, and I was relieved to be able to get back to Mansfield.

I only ever saw Doug again when he came home on leave (maximum length of 72 hours). He was not always able to let me know when he was coming home, but would send me a postcard (always censored by the authorities) on those occasions when he could. When our first child, John was born, Doug was allowed 4 8 hours leave to see him. The nurses at Victoria Hospital were extremely strict and only allowed Doug ten minutes with me and the baby before being told to leave. He only ever saw John on a very few occasions before being released from service at the end of the war.

The news of John's birth was passed on to my parents by our neighbour, Mrs. Harrop at 75, Layton Avenue. She received a telephone call from the hospital and was only too pleased to relay the good tidings on. She was one of only a few people who had a private telephone on Layton Avenue at that time. John was baptised at St. John's Church on 29th. January, 1944.

Doug was one of six brothers; four serving in the navy, one in the army, and one working in the coalmines during the war. All came safely through the conflict. I also had two cousins from Suffolk serving in the forces; Albert who was in the RAF, and Bill who was in the army. Unfortunately, Bill never returned home as he died whilst working on the infamous 'Burma Railway'.

A number of my female relations also served in the Land Army and another with the Salvation Army in London.

My father and mother were married during World War 1 and so had a good understanding of my feelings. Dad had served in the King's Own Yorkshire Light Infantry in that conflict and was wounded at Ypres,

At the start of the Second World War, he was working as a bus inspector for Truman's Buses (I think, they were based at Shirebrook) but was allocated other work by the Ministry of Labour and National Service. He was asked to work initially at Marks and Spencers and then as a wages clerk for Birmingham Small Arms Co. Ltd. at the Quortex, Sutton Road, Mansfield, where he stayed until the end of the war. He also assisted with the local Civil Defence.

My mother had suffered from pernicious anaemia for many years and needed regular injections to

Land Army girls, from Mansfield, working near Laxton.

counteract it.

[ED These injections were manufactured in America but when the war started the American firm gave permission for the injections to be manufactured in Britain under licence]

These were administered by Dr. Preston, her doctor from the time when she had lived at Mansfield Woodhouse.

Fred, my brother, worked as a shop assistant for the Irish Manufacturing Company on Church Street, and was also an ARP (Air Raid Precaution) volunteer before being called up in 1941. He then entered the army and served with the Sherwood Foresters in the Mediterranean area until the end of the war,

When I had recovered from the rheumatic fever I was given various jobs to do by the Ministry of Labour and National Service. My first job was as a post lady delivering mail in the Lord Street Area. I collected my mail bag at 6 o' clock in the morning at the main post office (entrance off White Hart Street), delivered the mail, and then went back for a second bag to deliver. I normally completed the second delivery some time in the afternoon.

I then had to leave the Post Office when I suffered a miscarriage. When I had recovered, I was sent to do munitions work at Whiteley's on Victoria Street. This involved some soldering on equipment destined for aircraft (but we were never told what the equipment exactly did!).

My life was changed when I gave birth to my first son, John, at Victoria Hospital on 14th December, 1943.

After about one year I returned to work again, this time as an usherette at the Grand Cinema, Mansfield. This was just evening work on weekdays only, This was my last wartime job. As well as receiving wages for the above jobs, I also received a weekly 'wives allowance' from the government whilst Doug was serving in the forces. This was supplemented by a voluntary contribution of 30s.0d, (£1-50) per month paid by Seal and Turners, Doug's employer at the time he was called up, and by a weekly baby allowance when John was born. Of course, some of this was handed over to my parents to help towards my upkeep.

Soon after the outbreak of war, the council removed the iron railings from the top of my parent's front wall together with their wrought iron entrance gate. The removal of similar non-essential ironwork was carried out throughout the district to enable the metal to be melted down for conversion into something more useful to the war effort.

I also remember that shortly after the declaration of war we were all issued with a National Registration Identity Card and a gas mask. This was followed by a ration book for some foods, even though food rationing did not really begin until early 1940. Rationing kept a control on the amount of food we could buy weekly, regulating the supply of bacon and ham, meat, butter, cheese, margarine, cooking fat, milk, sugar, preserves, tea, eggs and sweets.

I seem to recall that the food allowances varied dependent upon supplies available at the time, but it was normal to be allowed 4 oz. ham or bacon, 2 oz. butter, 2 oz. cheese, 3 pints milk (tins of dried milk came later), 8 oz. sugar, 2 oz. tea and one egg per adult per week. We had to register with shops of our choice, and I registered with Marsden's, top of Wood Street for groceries, Blythe's butchers, Rosemary Street for meat, and H. Askew and Son, dairymen, Ladybrook Lane for the milk. As well as paying for all these items, you handed over your ration book to the proprietor at the shop, and he clipped out the appropriate coupons. My first ration books were buff coloured (for adults) but when I became pregnant I was issued with a green ration book (for pregnant

FRIDAY, FEBRUARY 12, 1943.

EMPIRE CINEMA

WENT THE DAY WELL?

The GREAT INVASION DRAMA

Approximate Times of Showing   2.0   4.55   7.50

MONDAY, 15th FEBRUARY. (6 Days).   Continuous from 1.45.

A FILM FOR ALL, & NOT FOR THE MANY, TO SEE

——— ALSO ———

JOHN BEAL   WANDA McKAY
"ONE THRILLING NIGHT"
3.30   6.30

BRITISH MOVIETONE NEWS
1.45   4.35   7.35

WENT THE DAY WELL?

This film was the finest of all the patriotic propaganda films made during the war.
Snug little Bromley End seemed safe from World War II, and the villagers welcomed the lorry loads of Royal Engineers rolling onto their quiet green acres. They didn't know they were disguised German parachutists installing radar apparatus to disrupt England's entire network. Nor did they suspect their community leader was a traitor. But gradually they learnt the sinister truth and bravely fought the Nazi occupation at the highest cost of all.

women and children under 5) which supposedly allowed me to go to the front of the queue and gave increases, in the ration allowance of milk: to one pint a day and eggs to two per week.

I also went to the clinic at the top of St. John's Street every week for the baby's orange juice and powdered milk. On other very rare occasions I was also able to obtain rusks and cod liver oil,

Even though fruit and vegetables were never rationed, very little was available from the stallholders on Mansfield market, and we were encouraged to 'dig for victory' by the Ministry of Agriculture. Like many others we dug up the back lawn and grew our own vegetables (mainly potatoes and carrots) to supplement our diet.

Occasionally my parents were able to catch a train from Mansfield, and with two changes (at Nottingham and Bury St. Edmunds) were able to visit relations in Lavenham, Suffolk. The train network at that time was more extensive and the system seemed to work more efficiently than today!

As well as being pleased to see their relatives and friends, they were able to bring back a variety of fruit and vegetables grown in the much larger gardens available in that rural area of Suffolk. We were very pleased to have this extra food supply and I remember bottling and preserving plums, damsons, tomatoes and onions for winter use.

Sometimes word spread that some unrationed food usually in short supply may be available for sale, and I remember being part of a very long queue, four deep, waiting to buy sausages from Ripley's pork butchers on Nottingham Road (opposite the Victoria Hotel). I was amongst the lucky ones able to purchase four links of sausage!

I know that fish was unrationed but was very scarce, and I cannot recall buying any during the wartime period.

We received many tips, food facts and recipes issued by the Ministry of Food, and thinking back it was amazing what we could produce in the circumstances using dried eggs and powdered milk.

My bottled milk was delivered by a young lady in a horse and cart, and I also remember her delivering the milk on a hand drawn sledge during a period of deep snow. My parents had their milk from the Co-op and this was also delivered by horse and cart. I think the horses enjoyed stopping outside our house as we always ensured that there was a large bucket of water available for them to drink.

Clothes rationing was also introduced as the clothing industry had to concentrate on producing uniforms and other items for the armed forces. We were issued with a clothes ration book in which coupons (or points) were provided for a year, covering every item of clothing from underclothes to dresses, trousers and coats. However, I was able to buy sufficient small pieces of material from 'Reubens' stall on Mansfield market, and wool from Farrand's drapers on Rosemary Street to enable me to make the majority of John's baby clothes whilst nappies could be bought from the chemists.

I recall petrol rationing being introduced, but this did not affect us as we were amongst the majority of people who did not own a motorcar.

I cannot remember having problems buying general household goods at the start of the war, but they grew scarcer as it progressed. This resulted in the manufacture of utility designs of such items as clothes, shoes, blankets and crockery, and the introduction of the austerity regulations, which even stopped the manufacture of most toys. However, we were able to buy some unrationed items such as shoe polish and matches at Mrs. Townroe's local shop at the corner of Layton Avenue and Byron Street.

My parents' house had two coal fires downstairs and one in the main bedroom upstairs. The living room had its own black-leaded cooking range, and this was normally the only fire lit during the day to give us some warmth and a supply of hot water. However, on Sundays, the front room fire was also occasionally lit.

Coal was rationed, and we registered with Ince's, coal merchants on Westfield Lane. Like all coal merchants he also had an unlimited supply of 'ovoids' (made from coal dust). Both the coal and the 'ovoids' were packaged in thick brown paper bags and used to be delivered to our house by horse and cart, and then put into our coalplace.

Small quantities of coke sometimes became available at the old weighbridge near the gasworks. These were also supplied in thick brown paper bags and I occasionally used to collect a few of these bags in the baby's empty pram.

One of the first jobs for my father every morning was to clear the ashes out of the living room fire grate and to empty them outside to help form a path in the back garden. He then set up fresh paper and sticks on the grate, lit the paper with a match or cigarette lighter, and, when the wood was burning sufficiently, he would lay lumps of coal on top. Once the fire was established, a kettle of water would be put on the adjustable cast iron stand above the side of the fire and, when boiled, would be used for either a cup of tea or for washing purposes. We also liked to toast a slice of bread over the fire using an extending toasting fork. Although we had a small two-ring gas cooker the cooking range oven was used extensively for meals and baking our own bread. If the fire had to be left unattended we would put a protective wire mesh fireguard around it to help prevent sparks flying out into the room and landing on the peg rug lying in front of the hearth. Whilst linoleum was the main floor covering throughout the house, most rooms had 'peg' rugs which had been made by either my mother or myself.

In common with most houses of this period, the only toilet was located outside and 'round the back'. This meant that chamber pots were kept under the bed for any nightime 'emergencies'. There was no electricity lighting in the toilet and the walls and ceiling were whitewashed. To try to stop the pipes from freezing up in wintertime, sacking was wrapped around them and a little oil lamp lit to give some extra warmth. Sheets of newspaper were torn up into more manageable sizes for use as toilet paper.

When the war started we made our own blackout curtains for the house. These were made of a specially thick material which prevented light filtering out from the rooms and being seen by enemy planes at night. The effectiveness of the blackout used to be checked every evening by the local air raid warden on his patrol. Street lamps were not allowed to be lit and vehicle headlights and torches had to be specially cowled.

Although we had some electricity lighting at home (supplied through a 'bob' slot meter), we normally used candles or small paraffin lamps for lighting in the evenings. We were able to collect the paraffin in our own small can from Drabble's garage on Rosemary Street. My father also took the accumulators from his radio to this garage when they needed charging up.

The only times enemy action had any direct effect on our locality was when the air raid warning siren went off at night on a couple of occasions, both being when my parents were away. In both instances I sheltered under the stairs (in the 'bogey hole') with my baby, and took along our pet dog, Nell and the canary in its cage. I was able to hear the drone of planes overhead and was relieved when the 'all clear' sounded, I then had a cup of hot tea to calm my nerves and went back to bed with the baby, allowing Nell to stay in the bedroom in her basket and the canary's cage being left on the bedside table. I later found out that the first air raid was on Coventry, and the second on Sheffield.

THE Mansfield Advertiser
(THE MANSFIELD & NORTH NOTTS. ADVERTISER).

No. 3,602. FRIDAY, JUNE 14, 1940. (12 PAGES.) THREE HALFPENCE.

MANSFIELD GIRL SHOT IN BARRIER INCIDENT.

JOY-RIDE ENDS WITH TRAGEDY.

MOTORIST IGNORED SENTRY'S CHALLENGE.

These were the headlines of the Mansfield Advertiser for Friday June 14, 1940. It transpired that the driver of a car which failed to stop at a guarded barrier on Nottingham Road, near the junction with Derby Road, was fired on by a sentry, with fatal injuries being sustained to a young lady passenger, Miss Mary Elizabeth Smith, aged 20, of 47, Hibbert Road, Mansfield.

The car was being driven by Frederick P. Strutt, of Cambria Road, Mansfield. He and his three passengers were returning to Mansfield at about midnight on the previous Saturday night. The car drove through the barrier at about 40mph and was fired on by a member of the Local Defence Volunteer Corps who was one of the guards at the barrier. He was John Edward Sanders, of 60, Garnon Street, Mansfield. The bullet passed through the back of the vehicle and hit Miss Smith who was in the rear seat. The car stopped after the shot was fired. When it was realised that Miss Smith was injured, she was driven to Mansfield General Hospital, but was found to be dead on arrival. At the inquest, the District Coroner, Lieut. Colonel H. Bradwell, recorded a verdict of "justifiable homicide" and attached no blame to the sentry, who, he said, was only doing his duty.

Later on in the war I also remember seeing a large number of our planes flying over with accompanying gliders being towed along behind. Again, I did not know it at the time, but this was part of the 'D-Day' offensive.

Generally however, the day-to-day routine of life in the home carried on as normal throughout the war.

The periodic visit of the chimney sweep was a hectic occasion as we always had to remove any curtains, rugs and ornaments as well as covering the furniture with dust sheets before he started work. He would then set up his own sheets across the fireplace before starting to push the brush rods up the chimney until the brush head could be seen coming out above the chimney pot. No matter how many protective dustsheets he used, it always seemed that the clouds of soot falling into the fireplace were able to seep right throughout the room. Afterwards the rooms were cleaned by washing the painted walls and into, with the windows being washed with water into which a little vinegar had been added. The opportunity was also taken to 'beat' the rugs on the clothesline. Any other cleaning was done either by using our Ewbank sweeper or with a dustpan and brush.

Other regular cleaning jobs included sweeping the pavement at the front of the house and scrubbing the doorsteps every week. Monday was always 'washing day'. The dirty washing would be boiled in a 'copper', rinsed out in a 'dolly tub', and then put through a 'wringer'. Which was secured to a stout table. Care was always taken not to catch our fingers in the rollers of the 'wringer'. The clothes were then hung out to dry on the clothes line in the back garden, or hung up in the kitchen if the weather was unsettled.

The ironing was done with a solid iron heated up on the front of the open fire. After completing any jobs that needed doing I would occasionally do some knitting or embroidery for relaxation.

Sunday was always an important day for my parents who were both very religious, and they regularly attended the prayer meetings held at the Radford Street Gospel Hall located near to the Shoe Company factory. I also seem to recall that the Salvation Army band played hymns on the market place on most Sundays.

We tried to keep up with the progress of the war by listening to the B.B.C. radio broadcasts, and occasionally buying a national daily newspaper or local weekly newspaper such as the Mansfield Chronicle.

By 1945 it was realised that the war in Europe was drawing to a close, and we were overjoyed to hear the radio announcement of Germany's surrender to the Allies on the 7th. of May. Everybody seemed to pour out of their houses wanting to share the wonderful news, and I was eventually able to join the throng of happy people all converging on the town centre to celebrate. There was a mixture of happiness and relief as we listened to the bands playing whilst the church bells rang out in the background.

This was the culmination of over five years of war with Germany and I now looked forward to the safe return home of Doug and my brother Fred. Fred was the first to come home, but it was another eight months before Doug was discharged and allowed back. Even though this seemed to be a long time, I realised that others were still having to fight the Japanese, and that Doug was able to serve his time out in a now peaceful Europe.

It was further good news when Japan surrendered on the 14th. of August. The end of the war heralded a massive change for all the servicemen coming home, as they had to cope with their memories and a completely different way of life in 'Civvy Street'.

Evacuee who became my wife.
D.E. & I.E. Clarke

The family of George, his wife Ivy and daughter Irene lived in the East End of London, and at the outbreak of World War Two George was called up into the Army. He was in the Tank Corps serving in North Africa, and Ivy was working on Spitfires for the R.A.F.

As time went by London was severely bombed and after a while Ivy, having lost a sister in the Blitz, decided that she & Irene would 'go up North' for a rest. They arrived at Sutton-in-Ashfield by train, complete with lapel labels and gas masks etc, and were taken to a church hall to see if anyone would take them in. Finally a lady from the Carsic Estate - Mrs. Gladys Waring took Ivy and Irene to her home and looked after them both until they felt able to return to London.

Years went by and the war finally ended and happily George survived in spite of being wounded several times. George being the gentleman that he was decided to visit Mr & Mrs Waring in Sutton and thank them personally for looking after his wife and daughter. The two families struck up a long lasting friendship, and in 1958, on one of their visits to see 'Aunty Gladys' I was introduced to Irene and her family by Gladys's daughter Shirley and her husband Roy Beecroft. (We were members of The Mansfield Victoria Cycling Club). Immediately Cupid thrust his arrow of love and Irene and I were married in a bomb-scarred Church in the East End of London in the summer of 1960.

Irene still visits Aunty Gladys, now in her late 90's on a regular basis and my son Steven and I receive hand-knitted woollen socks from her each Christmas. Sadly Gladys's husband Fred and Irene's Mum and Dad are no longer with us, but the memories are still there of the kind people willing to help others in times of adversity.

Law and Order in Wartime Mansfield
Tom Gamble.

'Can I square you with a toffee?' wheedled Edith Edwards, of 66 West Gate, but P.c. Unwin was not to be sweet-talked and Edith was fined for breaching the Lighting Restriction Order. She was not alone. 39 others faced similar blackout charges at that October 1939 session of the Borough Magistrates Court in Mansfield and hundreds more followed over the next five years, thanks to the vigilance of the local A.R.P. Wardens.

Nor was it only the blackout that brought a massively increased number of charges before the Mansfield magistrates arising from the (estimated) 10,000 Special Orders under the War Emergency Powers Act. For the ordinary citizen trying to survive and the tradesman trying to make a living the law was a tangled thicket, often puzzling or threatening, sometimes seemingly absurd. Why, for instance, should it be an offence to 'cause fruit to be carried more than 40 miles.?' And what was so sinister about hens eggs marked with a red letter H that you could not buy them without a special certificate? And should a respectable Padley Hill butcher be hauled before the beaks for slaughtering a pig, his very own pig, just because it did not have a certificate from the Ministry of Food?

But these, along with the usual litany of petty crimes, were among the freshly minted offences to be dealt with by the Borough magistrates and a seriously over-stretched police force. Others included a wide range arising from the rationing and price restriction regulations and many hundreds of cases involving AWOL servicemen and civilians failing to attend satisfactorily, work to which they had been directed, especially mining, Home Guard training or fire-watching duties.

Beset by so many rules, restrictions and regulations, aggravated by the anxieties natural in wartime, family life showed the strains in the increasing flow of juvenile delinquency, bigamy and separation cases brought before Petty Sessions. With so much extra work to contend with, much of it of an unfamiliar character, the system did well to avoid collapse and perhaps deserves some belated recognition

My Memories of the War
Mrs Shore.

I lived on Central Ave. during the war. I was married in 1935, and had two young children (1937, 1941) so I did not go out to work. My husband was a miner, and an ARP warden.

We took evacuees. One was an expectant mother from Sheffield at the beginning of war. She stayed a week and then returned home. The second one was towards end of the war, and came from Worthing, she stayed for some months Also, near the end of war, we were about to go on holiday to Scarborough for 2 weeks when we were asked to take in family bombed out from London. We let them stay in the house while we were away. The evacuee family paid the rent. We also took in two Bevin Boys, (two others families on same street did too), one Bevin boy was from Aylesbury and we still keep in touch.

Because I had two young children I was not called upon to do any regular war work but I was involved in National Savings and went round my area once a week selling 6d. stamps. I was also involved in special efforts, eg. Such as the collecting of aluminium pans and iron railings all of which went to the war effort.

There was an air raid shelter in the road at end of Central Avenue it was brick built but became damp so it was little used.

The Princess Royal, Countess of Harewood, inspected Red Cross nurses and visited Mansfield General Hospital on 27 April 1944, escorted by Mr John Harrop White.

I saw wounded US soldiers brought in to Great Central Station, mostly in hospital blue, they were then taken to the US Army hospital at Kings Mill.

Royal Army Service Corps was billeted in town their nickname was 'the Rascals'. Their wives came to stay. I was a keen member of St. Peter's church and I helped in the canteen for soldiers at Grove House. We invited two soldiers back to our house for tea one cold wet October evening, unfortunately I only had two eggs, so I scrambled them and served four.

My penpal in Canada, sent us food parcels. Once she sent rice, sugar, tea plus a Tonka toy in a parcel, the toy ripped the bags and the rice and tea were mixed up, so we emptied it all onto the table and picked out the rice grains. We could not throw it away as we were very short of food.

I wasn't allowed to go to dances, so during my leisure time I did jigsaws, I read, wrote letters, and there was always knitting.

My Diary of the War Years
R. Sale

8.2.1941
There were queues everywhere, even in the Market and some of the people were not too good tempered. It is very difficult to get some things and if you are not early, it's all sold out. Some people will join a queue, even if they don't know what is being sold. One good thing is that bread is not scarce.

13.9.1941
I bought some fish, they called it 'Queen Wing', I paid 1/11 a pound. Never heard of this before. The queues are getting longer and nearly all of them are for non-essentials. We are the only country at war in the world where bread is not rationed.

8.11.1941
I bought a pair of shoes, 30shillings. (150p) I had to give 7 coupons, also some horseflesh for Biddy (dog), at 8d a pound uncooked and 9d a pound cooked.

25.12.1941
I gathered two rosebuds today. At Christmas Dinner we had no bird but something as good, English mutton with the usual plum pudding. This was the third Christmas Day under war conditions.

8.1.1942
I went into Mansfield to get fish for dinner, there was very little about. I got a meat pie at the butchers, 2s2d (11p).

9.7.1942
We got a letter this morning from Derrick. He was killed in action on June 17th in Egypt. It was very sad; the letter was full of hope and what he was going to do after the war.

11.7.1942
The Market Place was taken up with roundabouts, it being known locally as the Gooseberry Fair but gooseberries were conspicuous by their absence, nor were there any strawberries for sale. New potatoes were 6lbs for 1/-.

15.11.1942
Sunday, a lovely November day. The church bells were rung this morning, the first time since 1940, to celebrate the Allied success in the battle of Egypt.

18.2.1943
I went to a Ministry of Information's cinematographic lecture, a good programme of informative subjects. The first on 'sneezing' and how diseases can be spread, Inoculation of children against diphtheria; how to deal with an incendiary bomb; how the various services deal with a blitz; in the last, two German compositions which will last

forever - Hallelujah chorus and a Beethoven Symphony.

28.3.1943
At night we saw many bombers going south apparently on a raiding expedition. (I found out later it was to St. Nazaire, a port on the French coast.)

3.4.1943
Double British Summertime begins today, the clocks now two hours in advance of Greenwich.

26.4.1943
Ted has gone to Ripon in Yorkshire, to take a fortnight's Bomb Disposal Course.

16th May 1943
Today is the third anniversary celebrations of the 6th Mansfield Battalion, Notts. Home Guard in Berry Hill Park.

Officer Commanding W.H. Mein presided, the celebrations beginning with a Drum Head Service on the Chesterfield Road Park. His Worship the Mayor took the salute in the Market Place during the March Past.

In Berry Hill Park the Personnel of C. Coy Counter Marched to the Band of the 6th (Mansfield) Battalion. Various displays included wall scaling, house entry, Platoon attacking, supported by the R.A.F., bayonet fighting drill, a demonstration by Dispatch Riders, and gun drill. A display of weapons was mounted, Lewis guns, Browning guns. Auxiliary Bomb Disposal equipment, Mortars, Wireless and Signalling items, Anti tank mines, Grenades, and Sten guns.

All the roads leading to Berry Hill were crowded and it was a job to get into the grounds, with the congestion at the gates. I liked the Platoon Attack the best, which was supported by Lancaster bombers and Spitfires.

7.8.1943
Saturday, there was to have been a Fete and Gala in Berry Hill Park today in connection with the 'Stay at home Holiday' but the event was spoilt by continuous showers all day.

18.10.1943
Great activity with searchlights tonight.

17.11.1943
While I was on the allotment (corner of Lichfield Lane and Berry Hill Lane) a Council man asked me if I could do with some fallen leaves they had swept up from the roads. I took two cartloads which will make good manure.

17.1.1944
Sergeant Major Ashmore of the R.A., an expert at bomb disposal, came to Mansfield to give a lecture to the Mansfield Bomb Squad. He stayed with us a night.

13.2.1944
A boy, Richard Lines, of Patterson Place, Ravensdale found a cordite cartridge on Ling Forest today. He hit it on some iron railings, it then exploded. He later died from his terrible injuries.

7.3.1944
There were large numbers of bombers passing over in the evening, far more than usual.

8.3.1944
We heard today that 1,000 bombers were raiding Berlin last night.

7.4.1944
This afternoon, there were great numbers of planes towing gliders passing over.

6.6.1944
Heard on the wireless that the invasion had begun, more than 4,000 sea craft in the Straits and eleven

thousand aircraft in support.

15.6.1944
There was an ambulance train in the L.N.E.R. sidings today, probably with wounded from the invasion.

7.9.1944
Announced on the wireless that blackout conditions would be relaxed, all curtains except those of a flimsy nature, would be allowed. In case of air-raid warning blackout must be used. Fire watching is also discontinued.

9.3.1945
It was announced today that the Americans had crossed the Rhine.

19.3.1945
Queues do not get any shorter, there was no fish to be had, and I even had to queue for sausages.

13.4.1945
Winifred, Duchess of Portland opened a Pets' Clinic today. It was packed with animal lovers and one dog carried a basket of flowers in its mouth and presented it to the Duchess.

27.4.1945
It was announced today that the U.S.A. army had made contact with U.S.S.R. troops near Torgau on the Rhine.

7.5.1945
It was announced on the wireless that the Germans had accepted the Peace Terms of unconditional surrender. Mr. Churchill will give the news at 3 o'clock tomorrow, the King at 9 o'clock.

8.5.1945
V. E. Day!

10.8.1945
Welcome news, the Japanese have surrendered to the Allies.

15.8.1945
V.J. Day!

16th August 1945
Thursday, a day of thanksgiving and holidaying - after dark - bonfires and fireworks.

BOROUGH OF MANSFIELD.

CIVIL DEFENCE DUTIES (Compulsory Enrolment) ORDERS, 1941.

This is to Certify that F. E. POTHECARY, of 75, Forest Road, Mansfield, has been granted exemption from Enrolment under the above Authority, due to having voluntarily agreed to do 48 hours' Fire Prevention Duties.

ON BUSINESS PREMISES.   Section 6   Group A

This Certificate shall have effect so long only as the conditions under which it is granted remain unaltered.

Date 17th November 1941

Town Clerk.

War Time Reminiscences
J. Pollard

I remember how little my life was disturbed. They were busy, blissfully happy years, when I went to school, studied for exams, went to college.

Food
There were American food parcels. My mother would encase a whole tin of pork (Spam) in a lard and potato crust to make a delicious pork pie. All the men, women and boys dug for victory and we had wonderful vegetables and salads. We saved the butter and marge rations for putting on new potatoes and vegetables and we enjoyed dripping and lard toast. My sandwiches for school were new bread, Velveeta box cheese, egg (never a shortage on this), potted meat made at home, or jam also homemade.

The chip shops never closed, occasionally no fish but always plenty of spuds and we had corn beef fritters and scallops, potato slices fried in tripe fat which was sold in all the butcher's shops off ration.

Drama
During the late '30's, '40's and '50's there was a wonderful vibrant interest in drama. There were drama groups in every village, town and school. All those gifted people who formed E. N. S. A. during the war later enlivened the West End and began Drama Schools or became Drama Advisors to all the schools in the country.

The Bevin boys were sent to work in the mines instead of being sent to the armed services, they were, many of them from Public Schools and they loved acting. At 17 I ran a Dramatic Society in a small colliery village where the boys taught me a great deal about producing a play. Every night we made our own entertainment and put on melodrama such as 'Night Must Fall', or 'The Monkey's Paw' and a marvellous production of '1066 and All That' clothed almost entirely in cast off curtains and furnishings.

All through the war there were new cinemas going up, the Ritz on Chesterfield Road and the Strand at Warsop. The managers wore evening dress and it was lovely to feel the luxury of deep piled carpets and upholstery and to see the magic of the organ rise, playing music for our entertainment. We found at the cinemas warmth of central heating and brilliance of light that was unknown in our own homes. Our floor coverings were usually linoleum and rag rugs and we had oven shelves wrapped in blankets for hot water bottles. We had wireless but no T.V. and there were not many newspapers. We listened to the 6 'o clock news and we occasionally saw the Pathé News at the cinema.

The Impact of War
During the war I was at Teacher Training College, high up above the Wharfe Valley but near to Bradford and Keighley. There was a radio in the Students Common Room and we had the Sunday newspapers but we were so busy studying or preparing next weeks lessons for schools in Bradford we had no time to read or listen. We were rationed for food but there was always plenty. When I went to college many of the people in my home village gave me coupons for my necessary clothes. We heard the bombs and gunfire distantly and approaching the D Day landings could leave college only to walk on the moors where there were no signposts so we used compasses. The war was very far away.

In 1946, when I began teaching at HighOakham both the fire and air raid alarm were just where they had been installed at the outbreak of war and as far as I know they are still there. Miss Ullyatt, who taught History, told me of receiving the evacuees at the Bethel church and how all the people living on the little streets off Nottingham Road and Titchfield Park welcomed them with open arms - even though it meant their own children having to sleep 3 or 4 a bed. The Staff also talked of fire watching every night and the fun!! of staying in the Domestic Science flat. Some of the last evacuees were housed in a large white house on High Oakham Road because it had large attics, as it had been a barracks in Victorian times.

For me the War Years were for learning and looking forward. During the war our interests broadened and our horizons became more distant. Women had their own horizons broadened as they contributed to the war effort. Facing the challenges and finding themselves very capable of driving the lorries, manning the searchlights, making aeroplanes and tanks etc, running hospitals, and making decisions. They never went back to the kitchen sink for they had realised their worth and their strength and that they could and should make their own minds up.

Wartime Memories
Bob Renshaw

I was born on 21 Aug. 1931 so I was barely 8 when the war started. I believe that my father and my mother must have openly discussed their anxieties about the possibility of another conflict. So I did have some appreciation of what was going on and understood the excitement if not the fear when we listened to Mr Chamberlain's declaration of war on 3 Sept. Adult trepidation was tempered by the frequently exchanged belief, or hope, that 'it will all, be over by Christmas.' I certainly heard this voiced and it was only many years later that I realised the possibility of irony, having discovered the same optimism had been expressed in 1914.

A strange thing, considering my reading and access to adult thought, is that I had no idea what a Jew was. I do not think the word entered my consciousness or vocabulary until I was in my teens and someone commented, non-judgementally, that a class mate, whom I had known for several years, was Jewish. As he was perfectly ordinary in every way, apart from being red-haired and heavily freckled, it had no significance. I think that it was only after Belsen, Buchenwald and Dachau had been liberated that I became aware of Nazi anti-Semitism.

My first actual wartime memory is of the air-raid sirens. One had been located in the bell tower at my school. It must have been installed in anticipation of the war to come as there had been plenty of warning, because there was a trial sounding to ensure recognition. Then, to ensure alertness and to lower initial panic levels, a false alarm was sounded on the night of 3rd Sept. This woke me and I rushed to my parent's bedroom, overlooking the road, where we saw a mature woman, in nightdress and gasmask, running in the direction of Ling Forest. (An area of heathland some 2 or 3 miles east of Mansfield). Gas masks, like air raid sirens, must have been introduced 'just in case'. I believe that blackout curtains were an immediate requirement (I remember my mother making them and still using them as dust covers in the 70s and 80s). 'Put that light out!' was the cry of the wardens and 'Got your gasmask? Got our torch?' replaced 'Put your scarf on and button your coat' as a parting remark. My father, Sam, like his own father, was a hosiery framework knitter. He started work at thirteen at the mill on Hermitage Lane. When the Quortex opened, he and his father and three of his brothers moved there and remained for most of their working lives. The youngest brother became a cobbler. At the start of war the Quortex was managed by two Germans, Herr Damstedt and Herr May. The worst thing I heard said about them was that they not only ate liver sausage but also the fat which surrounded it. Before they were interned there were rumours of wireless transmitters in the lofts of their houses and tales of them meeting with other spies in the forest near Ollerton Corner.

All my father's younger brothers served in the armed forces - one of them contrived to fall off the gangplank and break his leg when embarking for the Far East. The youngest sister became a land girl, eventually marrying a GI and now living in Oregon. Although Sam was just young enough to have served, he failed the army medical. Consequently he was sent on war work repairing aircraft at Tollerton airport. The travelling, often in darkness, long hours and boredom made him a sick man but at least he was never shot at. His health soon recovered in peacetime. He never could see very well in the blackout and had a habit of walking into lamp posts and the like. Apart from the shifts at Tollerton, he was also recruited on fire watch which luckily for him took place in the chapel next door to our house (corner of Eakring Road / Normanton Drive).

As an avid newspaper reader, I found the war exciting. In particular, I recall the chase by the Ajax, Achilles and Exeter of the Graf Spee to Montevideo and later the subsequent capture of the German POW warship Altmark. Dunkirk was the next major event. Some troops were marched from the railway station to Carter Lane School where they were to be billeted. My mother took me up to watch them arrive, as she perceived it as an historic event. How much I remember and how much is from my mother's retelling I am uncertain, but they were a ragged, dog-tired bunch, some walking wounded, others assisted. But when the sergeant-major in command saw the waiting crowd, he called his men smartly to attention and they marched proudly past and into the school. Harry Radford immediately closed his barbershop on the corner of Argyle Street to the public and offered to give any soldier who wished a haircut and a shave for free.

When my mother told me that we would have to house an evacuee I asked that it be a boy named Bill. It turned out to be Raymond from Worthing, whose sister Hilda was billeted six doors up with the Speights - a family I had not known well but whose sons Trevor and David were to become my close friends. The visitors did not stay long and I have to say that they were resented rather than welcomed. If I remember correctly, Hilda and Raymond moved somewhere together. Southend moved into QEGS, this led to a morning/afternoon shift system for a short time. Before the war there had been only men teachers. This changed immediately, as all those young and fit enough were called up. But to maintain tradition it was decided that all the replacement women teachers should be addressed as 'Sir'. This seemed very strange at first but we adapted very quickly.

Food acquired a new importance during the war. Fond memories are of powdered egg, which made a strange foreign dish called 'omelette' which was solid and flat and delicious in a sandwich - and, towards the end, American sausage meat. This came in tall tins with a core of spicy minced pork surrounded by a half inch of delicious dripping that was lovely on toast. The only available cheese was 'mousetrap' which became greatly acceptable when fried and sandwiched with HP Sauce, the bread having been dipped in the residual pan fat. A British Restaurant was located on Belvedere Street. I recall eating there with my mother. I think we had some sort of pie, possibly Woolton pie, that I enjoyed.

My father was closely acquainted with a baker, Harold Harvey. They went to race meetings and dog tracks occasionally, frequently with greengrocers Tiny Roberts and Billy Gilbert. The latter delivered round the houses by horse and cart and at a time of transport difficulties the quartet decided to use this transport to go to Southwell Races. Unfortunately, the horse, also called Billy, stopped at every third house on Southwell Road and they never got there.

In the later years of the war, I walked with my friend Trevor Speight each Saturday morning to Harvey's bakehouse on Littleworth. We would always get a dozen currant buns, it seemed as if there was one currant per bun, and occasionally we had other more exotic treats. We were allowed to eat a currant bun each on the way home. We also kept a few chickens, for eggs and meat. I remember my father deciding to neck the cockerel. This proved difficult, as it was a very strong bird of evil temperament. Eventually it broke free but foolishly tried to reach the next door garden by squeezing through the gap in the fence slats. My father jumped the fence and pulled on its head until it gave up the ghost.

My Uncle Tom a joiner and therefore in a reserved occupation, was employed on various building projects throughout the area at airfields and other government installations. These were usually in rural areas and put him in a position to help farmers with the odd bag of cement or whatever in exchange for a few bags of sugar or a joint of pork. We would fairly frequently benefit from such gifts. Tom also built our air raid shelter. This was a pretty substantial affair, a single brick room, some 10 to 12 feet long by about 8 feet wide and six feet high. It was brick built, only single leaf we discovered, when it was eventually demolished, with a concrete roof reinforced with old iron bedsteads. Straight flights of brick steps led down to doors at each end. The shelter was shared with our neighbours, the Dickinsons, at the first house on Normanton Drive. George Dickinson ran a cable for electric light from his bird hut (a former railway carriage) and there were bench seats, which could be bridged to form beds when necessary, either side of the shelter. Six of us, occasionally seven, spent several full nights down there when Sheffield and Nottingham were being bombed. We could hear the bombers passing overhead, the Anti Aircraft guns and the occasional attack by fighters. I was allowed to go up and watch the glowing sky over burning Sheffield. The only real danger to us, I believe, was of bombers on their way home being brought down by our planes or dropping surplus bombs to lighten their load.

Later on in the war I remember watching the gliders being towed overhead on their way to the continent. Whether this was D-Day, or D-day +1, I cannot be certain.

Tom's own air raid shelter was the prototype for ours but, I think, with only one entrance, which seems a mistake. Other shelters I remember were the ones on the bottom field at school (QEGS) which were of brick, half buried in the ground and roofed with turf over concrete.

Early in the war, Johnny Leaf, who lived across Eakring Road from us, went missing on his way home from Carter Lane School one afternoon. He had taken a 'short cut' down Argyle Street, which led through to the Leaf's next door neighbours, Salmon's house and yard, on Eakring Road, and decided to jump into a public shelter which was being excavated. He was unable to climb out and was not found until dusk several hours later after a search by police and others. I also recall visiting the caves on the north side of Church Street which had been made accessible as public shelters early in the war.

On several occasions, I was persuaded, along with others, to help out in some way (cleaning rifles, sweeping floors) after school, at the Home Guard HQ, which I recall as being somewhere on Chesterfield Road. Our leader was the art/woodwork teacher Mr T. S. (Tim) Martin; he had the Home Guard rank of Major.

My closest teenage friend was Trevor Speight. His Uncle was in the Merchant Navy and would visit when home. I remember him bringing Trev and his brother David each a wooden sword made by the ship's carpenter. Trevor Speight and I took a bike ride down Eakring Road one day - presumably in the summer holiday-to Ling Forest, beyond Sherwood Golf Club. The heathland was criss-crossed with trenches from the Great War and served as an interesting playground. I found what was either a mortar bomb or an incendiary and took it home bouncing about in my saddlebag. When I showed it my mother she made me take it immediately down into the garden shed. She then sent a message to the nearest known Air Raid Warden who came and took it away, having warned me, and Trev. against

Boat Parade passing the Art Collage on Chesterfield Road.

touching anything similar again. On VE Day, Trevor and myself went down to Mansfield Market Place in the evening. It was thronged with people celebrating and just milling about and cheering as I recall. I think we stayed until about midnight which in those days that was late for 14/15 year olds.

My Wartime Memories
Miss. Wragge

When war was imminent I joined the A.R.P. On the Sunday war was declared I was at a lesson for A.R.P. at Carter Lane School and the caretaker of the school came and wrote WAR on the glass door. I had certificates for the various aspects of fire fighting I passed. We did our incendiary training at Toothill Lane in the Old Fire Station.

My A.R.P. duties were for two hours at High Oakham School usually from 8.00 - 10.00 when the regulars went off. The regulars were the two Mr. Bingleys and a Mr Warsop as well as the Maltbys. On the first Sunday the siren went 3 times and we were all called out on patrol in case we were needed.

One night we were on duty and went onto the Recreation Ground of High Oakham where we saw the bombs falling on Sheffield.

Leaving or Entering Mansfield

If you wanted to leave Mansfield in the evening you had to start out before 5.30 because after that time there were Specials posted at the exits of the town like Stockwell Gate, Robin Down Lane, Nottingham Road. They stopped all people going in or out of Mansfield, asked to see your Identity Cards and asked you where and why you were going.

Evacuees

I have no recollection of evacuees except of a Mr. English from London, who was a manager of a Pretty Polly firm; he lodged with my Aunt May on Hermitage Lane for the duration of the war and worked at Sutton.

Rationing

This didn't have a great impact on me as my mother dealt with all this. I do remember that we had rabbit for Sunday dinner. Our local shopkeeper always told us when bananas were in the shop. My Mother used to buy a cowheel and shin beef or pork and make brawn with them. We bought 3 piglets and kept them at the sties of the Plough Inn. You had to have a licence to kill them and one went to the Government, one was divided up between us and one was sold. I think it might have gone to Pork Farms as my brother worked there to be made into pork pies. My mother made black pudding from the blood.

I worked at the Grand Theatre, as Cashier for 40 years, and can remember the ice-cream was rationed as well as sweets but we managed reasonably well.

Coupons

I cannot remember any problem with clothes and coupons.

Entertainment

When war was declared all the cinemas and theatres were closed for several days. We opened the following Saturday with John Wayne's 'Stage Coach'. We had no trouble in obtaining films during the war and the cinema was very popular.

Mr. Robinson was the Manager of the Grand Theatre during the war and he arranged many benefit concerts for the R.A.F. Benevolent Fund. We had Elsie and Doris Waters I think and also Ethel Revill and Gracie West. We also had the Nottingham Palais Band Leader, Mr. Billy Merren who waived his fee because his resident singer, Miss Lita Rosa, I think, had a new song to perform and he felt that, as it was a winner, it would more than repay him, as indeed it did. I have a feeling that Joan Hammond came twice during the war.

VE Day

When victory in Europe was declared a great party was held outside the Grand. We sang and danced until 4.00am and then some of us went into the Horse and Jockey, run by Mr. and Mrs. Sherrif at that time, as they had opened early.

Remembering the War
Mr. Bullick

Fortunately we lived in a part of the country which escaped the horror of bombing. Apart from seeing occasional tanks and, later in the war, observing scores of our heavily laden aircraft circling in the evening skies to gain height prior to bombing raids on Germany, we lived a life of relative normality. During the war years there was a constant stream of exhortations of what we were to do, or not to do. National Savings weeks urged us to purchase Savings Certificates, "Dig for Victory" campaigns stressed the importance of growing food, whilst various posters told us to "Save Electricity" or "Save Water" (by using 4 inches of water for a bath). Other posters proclaimed "Walls Have Ears" and "Careless Talk Costs Lives" and were intended to remind people of the danger of openly discussing anything of military importance. All of this propaganda, together with the daily experience of living in a 'rationed society', quickly shaped one's attitude to the importance of economy.

My five years at the local Grammar School more or less coincided with the war years and were reasonably happy, my most abiding memory of school being the watery custard that was served on our dessert at lunch time. (This invariably seemed to be either prunes or steamed pudding — but there was a war on!) My mother used to collect peoples' contributions for National Savings during the war years. To the best of my knowledge she used to sell 6d stamps which were stuck into a National Savings Book and eventually converted to National Savings Certificates when the subscriber had amassed a total of 15/-

During the war my family lived at Stanton Hill. Soldiers were billeted at Hardwick Hall (I think these were paratroopers.) and I can remember going and looking for spent ammunition cases on the firing range where the troops practiced. Whilst on one of these visits to Hardwick I acquired a small piece of the fuselage of a Boulton-Paul Defiant night fighter which had been shot down during a German air raid. My brother who, in the early 1940's worked at Silver Hill Colliery, Teversal as a junior Surveyor, recalled that after a night out in the vicinity of Mansfield or Sutton-in-Ashfield the paratroopers would steal bicycles from the cycle shed at the colliery, ride the mile or two down to Hardwick Hall and then dispose of the bicycles into the lake in Hardwick Hall grounds.

Rationing was immediately introduced in the war years and everything was in very short supply. Tea, sugar, meat, bacon, eggs, butter and margarine, cheese, and milk were all on ration but this ensured that everyone received a basic supply of essential food and it did not go to only those who could afford to pay exorbitant prices, it was not uncommon for housewives to have built up stocks of sugar and tins of various descriptions to supplement the rations which they were allowed. When shopkeepers had supplies of a more luxurious nature, such as tinned salmon, these would be produced surreptitiously and sold to their more favoured customers with the instructions that these be quickly concealed amongst their more mundane purchases. Although food was rationed it is probably true to say that as a nation we were fitter then than we are now in more affluent times and housewives were very adept at making wholesome meals out of a very few ingredients. Lord Woolton was the name of the Minister of Food and he will long be remembered for the Woolton Pie, which was named after him, this was a vegetable pie, which could be prepared from whatever vegetables were in season.

When people got married it was not uncommon for the bride's family to donate clothing and food coupons in order to purchase the items required for the ceremony and most three tier wedding cakes of the time had two false tiers which were made from cardboard. There were no bananas, oranges or lemons imported into the country during wartime and children who had never seen these fruits were completely bemused as how to peel a banana when they finally became more plentiful. I can remember that bottles of concentrated Orange Juice were produced for expectant mothers and young children. Furniture too was in very short supply and new furniture which bore the 'Utility Mark' was only for newly married couples and those who had lost their possessions in air attacks.

I remember when we lived at Stanton Hill just after the Dunkirk evacuation the troops who returned were housed in Church Halls, schools and requisitioned houses. We had two troopers come to our house for Sunday tea and I can remember one of them, who was from Canada, gave me a prayer book which he had with him in France. My future wife, who lived with her family on Carter Lane, Mansfield, remembers that the troops who came from Dunkirk occupied Carter Lane Junior School Hall. The pupils were taught at St. Lawrence's Church Hall for a few days until the troops went.

She also recalls her father obtained the substantial old lift from the Co-Op in Mansfield and installed it as an Air Raid shelter in their garden at Carter Lane, Mansfield. It was used only once for this purpose because of the relative absence of bombing in the area and also because of the dank earthy smell when inside. It was fitted out with food, candles, etc. and had bunks on which one could sleep if desired. She also remembers that there was a larger Air Raid Shelter situated on Argyle Street, off Carter Lane and there was also one on Scarcliffe Street at the bottom of Skerry Hill. These were much larger than the Anderson Shelters, which only housed a family. They were of brick construction with a concrete flat roof, and presumably were intended to protect people from shrapnel during Air Raids. There were many similar examples of this type of shelter scattered around various streets and all invariably smelled of damp. Because there was no need these shelters were certainly not used for purposes of air raid protection in this area.

Her father was a sergeant in the Home Guard and was on one occasion engaged on an exercise involving the protection of part of Mansfield from invaders. She was out on her bicycle and saw some men in military uniform with blackened faces crawling along a railway embankment and immediately told her father. As a result these 'invader' were quickly captured and thereafter she was credited by her father as having saved Mansfield from the enemy.

The American forces were situated in at King's Mill, (I think it was chiefly a Hospital) which is now the site of the busy modern hospital and after the war some of the Nissan huts next door were used as a school for the Mansfield Junior Technical School later to become Sherwood Hall Comprehensive before it was built on its present site. The Head Master was Mr. Palfreyman, who had previously taught at Brunt's School and later served with the RAF.

Dig for Victory campaigns were frequently advocated and everyone was encouraged to have allotments and cultivate any piece of land which would help the war effort. My wife recalls that St. Lawrence's vicarage on Shaw St., Mansfield possessed tennis courts which were dug up and used for producing vegetables. People were also encouraged to keep hens and rabbits and I believe that the provision in the deeds of some houses which specifically prohibited this was waived during wartime.

It was not uncommon practice for the houses that had been built in Victorian times to have low brick garden walls surmounted by iron railings. These railings disappeared round about 1942 when they were cut down and presumably taken away to be used to assist the war effort. Evidence of this is still visible to day on the garden walls of some streets of old houses. There was also the collection of aluminium pots and pans which, ostensibly, were for the production of aircraft, but whether or not these items were suitable for, or ever used for this purpose, remains a debatable question.

Evacuation was introduced as soon as war was declared and I remember, living at Stanton Hill and having a young girl stay with us from Birmingham as an evacuee. After a few weeks she returned to Birmingham. My wife remembers that they had an evacuee called John Howe from Leigh-on-Sea stay with them at their house for quite a long period. Her brother, who went to the Queen Elizabeth's Grammar School for Boys, remembers that he attended a long morning session, while the evacuees went for a similar period in the afternoon. I recall that in my form at Brunt's were the two Mostyn brothers, Peter and Brian, who had been evacuated from Southend-on-Sea and they were here for a considerable period. I think that a lot of the evacuees returned to their homes when it became apparent that the scale of air raids on their neighbourhood was not as large as had at first been feared.

Holidays were non-existent during the early war years and the only ones which I had consisted of returning to my grand parents in the North East of England, from where we had moved in 1938. Beaches were covered with barbed wire entanglements and other defences against invasion and seaside resorts were devoid of holiday makers. This state of affairs persisted during the first stages of the war, but I remember in 1943 that my mother, accompanied by my elder brother and sister, spent a week on holiday at Blackpool. A chance meeting, by my brother in a bar, with another young man resulted in the later meeting of my sister with this stranger and they have recently celebrated 55 years of marriage. The Government were very aware of the effect of absence of holidays on the population and were instrumental in getting local authorities to put on 'Holidays at Home' weeks, where various attractions were organized for the benefit of holiday makers.

Right from the start of the war a strict 'blackout' was imposed. This resulted in housewives having to line existing curtains with black material, if they were not of sufficient thickness; while the more sophisticated handymen constructed wooden frames covered with roofing felt, which were then fixed onto the outside of windows at night. Any chink of light exposed would result in the shout of 'Put that light out' from ARP (Air Raid Precaution) Wardens who looked out for any violation of the blackout. Motor vehicles too were required to have adaptors on their head-lamps which resulted in a very poor beam shining only upon the road. In those days ownership of a car was most unusual and because of the very stringent rationing of petrol most private cars were laid up during hostilities. Most of the vehicles on the road were Public Transport or military with a very few commercial lorries and vans.

'Fire watching' was also introduced early in the war, where observers of an area would give early warning to the AFS. (Auxiliary Fire Service) of any fires resulting presumably from the use of incendiary bombs by the enemy. I remember that my sister, who was employed at Sutton-in-Ashfield UDC offices, occasionally used to have to go and spend a night on this duty. It was a joke in the family that the only fire she watched was the one providing heating in the post where she was situated. Like most things this duty tended to die out in those parts of the country which did not experience enemy action.

An Evacuee from Worthing
Paul Tee

The war, as I remember it, started as a 7 year old, walking down our road one morning to post a letter for my parents, when the milkman said to "Hurry home, there's a war on".

My father, owing to his age and a slight touch of rheumatism too, became a War-Reserve Policeman.

I also remember seeing a large crocodile of children and grown-ups coming down our road and my parents saying 'the evacuees are coming'. Little did I realise that I would be in the same situation myself the following year.

Our next door neighbour had a mother and daughter billeted with her, whose father, as I was told, was a fireman in London in the East-End dock area. The house on the other side was empty at the time, as the couple who lived there had both joined the forces.

I remember the Battle of Britain over our skies on the south coast, watching the planes wheeling high in the sky and trying to shoot each other down.

At this time, my father being in the police force, decided I would be evacuated with the other kids from our school. I remember being on our local railway station, on Wednesday, 19th March 1941, with a small case, a gas-mask and a small label tied to me. I had no idea where we were going, but I do remember a large steam train that was going to take us there.

When we arrived at Mansfield Woodhouse we were taken to a large hall and given some food. We slept on mattresses on the floor. The next day we were taken in groups to be billeted on the locals.

We shuffled along Station Street and into Castle Street. Each door was knocked on, and someone left our ranks. When we got to number 15 a lady came to the door, and it was my turn. I entered a whole new world, and a whole new environment, which came as a shock to me.

I came from a semi-detached house that was only five years old, all electric and gas, with hot and cold running water, and a bathroom too!, to a terraced house with only cold water on tap, and gas lighting on the ground floor only.

The family who lived there were a Mr. and Mrs. Ernest Mason. They had two sons, Albert and George. Mr. Mason was a foreman at the mills, Albert was a few years older than me, and George was in the army. I don't think George and I ever met.

It was a very clean and happy house, but for us coming from the South of England, to live in a village where everybody worked in the coalmines and woollen mills, it might as well have been a foreign country. The language was different, the food and environment was very different.

I think most of us went to Yorke Street School, and of course we seemed to have a higher education for our age. That didn't seem to help much; our accents didn't either.

Mind you, I must add that 15 Castle Street was a happy house to live in once you got used to it.

In those days the milk came by horse and cart, in churns, and you collected it in a jug. Also, the coal arrived the same way outside the front door. It had to be carried through the house to the coal shed at the back. Whereas at home the milk came in bottles and the coal by the sack, and put in the coalbunkers.

The house was very dark as the windows were small, and opposite there was a very high wall of the Manor House. Over the wall grew a very large Mulberry tree, and we picked and ate the fruit in the

Autumn.

My first Sunday lunch, I will always remember. We all sat at the table and I had a plate of Yorkshire pudding with onion gravy. I asked where the meat and veg. were and I was told that this came later — this was most unusual to me.

I remember the range in the living room, with the oven on one side, the fire in the middle, and the boiler for hot water on the other side. The tin bath was put in front of the fire on Friday nights. I remember the smell of fresh bread, as Mrs. Mason baked her own twice a week. I remember going off to the Co-op in the High Street to carry home large bags of flour to make the bread. I remember the large copper in the scullery where the washing was done, and the stone stairs up to the bedrooms that were worn down over the years. I remember taking a candle to bed, the outside toilets that were in the back yard, and the old newspapers cut into squares hanging from nails.

Recreation time was spent in the park at the top of Castle Street, on the swings and slides. I remember having a swing hit me in the face and being taken to a doctors in Church Street, and being stitched. I've still got the scar on my cheek today.

Sunday afternoons we were sent to Sunday School, but we went to the park and listened to the band instead.

There were some allotments up the Vale Road on the right, near where the buckets went over the road from the mine to the slag heap. Further up the Vale Road we picked peas for a shilling a bushel. We used to go to the Tivoli Cinema on Saturdays.

Further up the High Street at Albert Square we had a meal at a British Restaurant each week.

On the corner of Castle Street and Station Street there was a shop that sold bottles of pop and ice cream. A little further down was the tripe shop. I went there to get some pig knuckles for Mrs. Mason one day. The lady behind the counter was stoking the fire at the time, and she cut off some tripe for a customer and left sooty fingerprints on it. It's funny how small things stick in your memory.

My parents visited me for a few days to see how I was, and they told me years later that they had never seen such good quality bed linen on their four-poster bed. I think that I returned home after about 9 months.

The return home was a complete contrast. We had tape on our windows, the blackout was much more strict, and the air-raid sirens were going quite often.

Back at our old school we were trying to catch up to our old standards, and everyone was trying to adjust. They were trying to get us to talk and lose the odd words that had entered our speech.

My parents kept in touch with Mr. and Mrs. Mason over the years and I remember visiting them again when I had my motorbike at sixteen. I last saw Albert and his wife some three or four years ago when I was staying with my cousin at Nottingham.

During my last visit I showed my wife the old mills at the top of Vale Road, which were now derelict. I was remembering how Mr. Mason had shown my parents and I round the mills 50 years earlier. I had stood outside and could hear the noise and clanging and banging of all the machinery in the vast buildings. Now, the only person I saw as I stood by the waters edge was walking a dog, and all I could hear was silence.

On one visit I parked my car where 15 Castle Street used to be, it is now a car park. I remembered as a small child of 9, walking up that narrow road with suitcase, gas-mask and label.

BOROUGH OF MANSFIELD

PEACE DAY CELEBRATIONS AND CARNIVAL

1939   1945

THE MAYOR
(Councillor C. Brown)

THE MAYORESS
(Mrs. C. Brown)

SATURDAY
SEPTEMBER 22nd
1945

SOUVENIR
PROGRAMME
Price Sixpence

All Profits from Sale of this Programme go to Mansfield Hospital £50,000 Appeal.

VE Street Party on Bould Street.

I remembered the smell of fresh bread, a bag of chips for a penny, the old Tivoli where we booed and cheered the villains and heroes on the silver screen, the clanging of the buckets on their way to the slag heaps, turning the mangle in the back yard for the washing, the colliery band in the park, and the town centre seemed so small now.

Two Memories kept Secret
J L Noble

One summer day in 1942, when I was 16 years old, I was enjoying a bike ride in the Nottinghamshire countryside. As I rode along Longdale Lane, I heard a growing engine noise, and an aeroplane flashed past at hedge-hopping height, then vanished. I was not surprised by it, as I knew that Rolls-Royce used Hucknall Aerodrome which was only two or three miles away. But I went weak at the knees when I suddenly registered that the 'plane I had seen - had no engine!

(Ed. – it's usually – no propeller! when the early jets first appeared.)

Being well-drilled by government propaganda ('Walls have ears', and 'Careless talk costs lives'). I kept my experience to myself. But I had many uneasy moments before the news of Whittle's jet engine was made public.

Continuing my ride, I soon had my attention caught by flashes of silver in the roadside grass. When I looked closely, I found the cause was strips of paper about 8" long, black on one side and silver on the other. I felt certain that they were connected with flying and the war. I took some home, but it was a long, long time before I learned that they were code-named 'windows' and were dropped from aircraft to confuse enemy radar detection. I now only have one strip left, a precious relic to remind me of a memorable bike ride into history.

My War Years
Russ Yeomans

I was almost eight years old when war was declared in 1939. At the time I did not realise what it was all about until the first few nights, when we were dragged out of bed and made to sit under the stairs by candle light in what we called the 'glory hole' after the sirens had gone off. This was not the most comfortable of situations so, after a few nights of discomfort and sleep deprivation, it was realised that a bomb dropping on Pleasley Vale was a very remote possibility and we all returned to our beds.

Pleasley Vale is a small village between Mansfield Woodhouse and Pleasley which consisted of three rows of cottages. We lived in the bottom row at number 24. The middle row was where the shop and the post office were and the top row had the best views. The village was owned by William Hollins whose three woollen mills were just a little further up the road towards Pleasley. The cottages were tied, so you had to work at the mills to be housed in them. The village was surrounded by woods and the River Meden passed through, in fact about twenty feet from our front door. You can imagine this was an ideal place for a young boy to live and grow up in.

The war began to have an effect on me when six of my cousins from the village were called up. Three from one family went into the navy, two went into the air force and one into the army. My father, though eligible, was exempt because he was in a reserved occupation as they turned some of the mills into a munitions factory.

Early on in the year the military descended upon the village in the form of a searchlight battery. They set up their canvas camp on the eastern side of the cricket field. The searchlights and generators were situated next to the pavilion. This meant that we kids were never far from this newly acquired interest, especially at the soldier's mealtimes. After they had completed their meal we were often given what was left. You can imagine our delight at being seated at a table in the mess tent and being given a mess tin, some fifteen inches square, with rice pudding in it an inch and a half thick and being told to get stuck into that.

Shortly after the search light battery went they turned what we called the 'sidings', which was a big stone building with a railway line running through the centre, into a storage depot. This building was next to the cricket field.

The next things to arrive were jerry cans; they came in their thousands and were stacked once again on the cricket field in neat heaps some twenty feet square and twelve feet high. They were all sheeted down which made it difficult for us kids to climb on but it wasn't for the want of trying.

Whilst the jerry cans were still stacked there the next items to arrive were the large 'Diamond T' tank transporters, thanks, I think, to the Lease Lend Pact. They were parked nose to tail right through the village. I believe they came to collect ballast weights which were delivered into the sidings by rail. The weights would give them stability when towing their trailer with a tank on.

We had some of the soldiers who were stationed at the sidings billeted with us as did several families in the village, because about a dozen of the houses in the row were three stories high and had four bedrooms so space was never a problem. We had a sergeant from Sheffield and after he had been here for a while his wife and children came here to get away from the bombing. This helped with the family income and, certain foodstuffs arrived which were never part of our rations, if I ever inquired where they came from I was soon told to mind my own business which I did!!

Number One Mill, which was the one nearest Pleasley, had part of it turned into either the manufacture or assembly of anti-tank guns. These guns were tested on a piece of ground just past the mills, off what we called the Black Pad. This was a cinder track which met up with the Pleasley to Shirebrook road. The army erected a large Nissan hut without any ends and the chap who tested these guns would set up, aim at a target and fire. He would have earplugs to suppress the noise but we kids, who were allowed to stand outside and watch, could only hold our hands over our ears and, I have to say, the blast from these guns when fired was quite an experience.

In addition to the three rows of cottages in the village there was a large house called The Uplands. This house was situated on the top of the rocks at the back of the middle row and was owned by the Royce family who, at the time, owned Mansfield Shoe Company. They had two sons, Michael and Barry, both of whom were in the R.A.F. We were told that they were attached to Rolls Royce as test pilots testing the engines after they were fitted in the planes, whether this was true or not I don't know but, I do know, that from time to time one or the other of them would come over the village either in a Spitfire or Hurricane and give a flying display which had to be seen to be believed. Swooping down to tree top height doing rolls and loops and waving to us as he passed. You can imagine the effect this had on us kids, everyone was going to be a pilot!!

Thursdays was a good day because the Hotspur and other comics were delivered. We read them with great interest and, at the earliest opportunity, re-enacted all the heroic deeds of the fictional characters in the woods.

During the war we were told to 'dig for victory' and every household in the village had the opportunity to do so by owning an allotment. It took up a lot of my playing time to have to keep the fire alight in the greenhouse when it was cold and, then having to go and open the door and windows when it was hot in summer, bearing in mind that these allotments were about half a mile from the house. Another task I had to undertake was to go in the fields and collect sheep manure, this was then put into hessian sacks and dropped into water butts, after this had soaked for some time the liquid was then fed to the tomatoes and everything else that needed feeding. Each year of the war Hollins paid a local farmer to plough and ridge part of one of his fields, as near to the village as possible. This was called the 'fallows' and everyone in the village was allowed two rows, they were numbered and marked with your name and then, at planting time, you had to set them with potatoes and, at the back end, dig them up. This was usually a family chore, dad used to dig up the spuds, mother, my elder sister and I would collect them in buckets then put them into four or five large sacks depending on the size of the crop. These would last us through the winter. We didn't have a wheelbarrow so dad's bike was used, one sack through the frame and one over the crossbars. Two or three trips were needed to get the potatoes home.

The war, to youngsters of my age, was never taken seriously and the thought of losing never came to mind and apart from incidents I have previously described it was just flags on a map in the school room. We were deprived of some things like chocolate and bananas but we always had vegetables.

We also bred rabbits for the pot so we lived pretty normally, and the black market was always around for items that were scarce. What I do remember about that time of my life was that the summers were very hot and we always had deep snow in the winter.

Crazes were always going on in school like collecting military cap badges or buttons or pieces of shrapnel. I have to say I enjoyed myself at school and, when the war in Europe was over, we had a great street party to celebrate.

A Soldiers View of Mansfield
W H Jackson

I was a member of the local regiment the Sherwood Foresters, 'C' Company, based in the old Drill Hall, Mansfield.

Although I worked in the mining industry I was called up for active service on the 28th August 1939. The mining industry was a very strong vital industry, providing coal for every steam driven ship, railway and other industry. Whiteley and Boneham's factories provided wireless components, while Metal Box (formerly Barringers) made gas masks.

The people of Mansfield and District suffered a terrible blow in April 1940, when the local 8th Battalion Sherwood Foresters was sent to Norway to fight the German Army who had invaded Norway. Our troops, who were well clothed for the cold country, were no match for the better equipped German Army. "C" Company lost some men killed and many were taken prisoner. The people in the district were very upset, but the war went on.

People had to get used to petrol, food and clothing rationing. My wife and I married on October 18th 1941. I left my wife after the wedding and the next time I saw her was July 1945 as I was in the Far East.

My wife never wrote in her letters to me about any troop movements, but when I came home in 1945 she told me stories of the American troops in Mansfield. The American Service pay was based on the cost of living in America, which was more than the cost of living in England, so the Americans had loads of money and could buy anything in Mansfield. They were the rich men in the Services. Of course our fellows were very envious, as our wages and pay were very low indeed. The Yanks attracted the girls locally, with chocolates and money. My wife said that when the Americans landed in Mansfield there seemed to be a little more food around. The popular meat was SPAM, obtainable only with your ration coupons.

When the D-Day landings had taken place, wounded and sick American servicemen and women came to the hurriedly built King's Mill Hospital in 1944. The Ambulance Trains were shunted into railway sidings at the Midland Station, all in full view of the workers in Whiteley and Boneham's factories, who, of course, during their lunch time break used to go and wave to the soldiers as the trains pulled in, and, even though the soldiers were injured, they threw chocolates and cigarettes to the English women.

What I have said about the American troops is only what my wife has told me, because there were no American troops in Mansfield before I went abroad in 1941, and there were none when I came home in 1945. Without the Americans we could not have won the war.

My mother had a young boy as an evacuee from London. He was aged 6 years. He went to the local school, but as soon as it was safe he wanted to go back to his parents. My father used to breed rabbits, and he was allowed a ration of meal to feed them provided he sold his surplus to the butchers, who in turn sold the meat to the general public.

Queues were an absolute necessity, especially if certain stores sold a little luxury like biscuits or beer, but the longest queue was for TRIPE OIL! Although the smell was awful, it was the one way you could get some fried chips. The oil was not harmful to health.

The war was not good for anyone, and even for those people who did not fight in the forces it was a miserable long time for civilians who had to live on rations. Vegetables were grown on gardens. Yeoman Hill Park, Mansfield Woodhouse, was ploughed up and food grown on it.

Snippets of Memories

Ambulance
Drivers were stationed in a corrugated iron building on Baums Lane where B. &Q. car park is now. We did 24 hours on and 24 hours off. We were able to rest in a house on Baums Lane, fully clothed and dash back if the siren went. We took soldiers (sitting patients) from Harlow Wood Hospital to Epperstone Manor or Lound Hall, speed about 30mph. Ambulance Attendants were stationed at the bottom of Gilcroft Street on Church Lane.

There were also Gas Decontamination Exercises on Sunday morning and in the week First Aid Classes. Some of the ambulances were what were called by some as 'sit up and beg' and the gears were gate change, others were American cars converted to take sitting patients.

Shelters
Halfway down on the right side of Handley's Arcade there is a door and a set of steps go up but, behind a closed and locked door, in the same location there are steps going down into caves that were to be used as shelters if needed.

Mrs Fearn
An Air Raid shelter was in the playing field behind St. Philip's Church, Westfield Lane, and there was an air raid siren at the old fire station.

Mrs Gent
There was an air raid shelter in the field (now flats) near a big house (Pedley's), at the corner of Methuen Ave/Gordon Ave.

Mr. Hall
There was an air raid shelter in Newgate Lane School playing fields.

D.A.Clay
In most of the streets in the town concrete, flat

roofed, blast shelters were erected for use by the townspeople in the event of air raids, this was done under the guidance of the Air Raid Wardens and Shelter Marshals.

POW''s
Mrs Fearn
I think there were Italian POWs working in the wood yard on Chesterfield Road

Mrs. Wright
Italian POWs worked on Bingham's Farm, Bleakhills Lane.

D. Smith also Mrs Shore
There was an Italian POW camp where Morrison's is now and they worked in the fields. It became the site of The Junior Technical School which later, on a new site, became Sherwood Hall Comprehensive.

M. Hall
It was said that German POWs worked at Barringer's as toolmakers!

D. A. Clay
There was a German POW camp at the Worksop side of the Carburton / B6034 Ollerton / Worksop road. The Italian prisoner of war camp was close by. Another Italian POW camp was between Caunton and the A1 trunk road.

Mrs Wright (nee Hallam)
In the 1940's I was a young girl living in Beeton's Cottage, Bleak Hill Lane, Mansfield. Whilst there, Italian POWs from their camp next door to the US Army Hospital at Kings Mill, would pass by on their way to work in the fields. One day I approached a group of Italians and asked for their autographs and they obliged.

Mr. Taylor
I can remember German POWs working on farms, and an Italian POW camp.

Army - British and American
Mrs. J Fearn
Aftermath of Dunkirk - The soldiers arriving in rags by train and truck, locals provided them with clothes and blankets

I remember the billeting of soldiers on Terrace Road with the Redcaps in Clifton Hotel. Palais de Dance was used for meals for the soldiers. My uncle was sometimes on sentry duty at Harlow Wood Hospital.

The Elizabethan - 1944
Congratulations to Sergt. R. Jephson (29-32) on receiving with due ceremonial in Rome, the Soviet Medal for Valour, together with documents authorising remarkable privileges. He is entitled to a life pension of 10 roubles (about 10/-) a month, to be claimed at any Soviet Embassy. He is provided with a special identity card which gives him the life-time privilege of free travel on Soviet territory by train, tram, or bus, also free admission to Russian places of entertainment. It now may be revealed that Sergt. Jephson was dropped behind the German lines in Jugo-Slavia to work with Tito's partisans. He spent over a year there and kept radio contact with the allies, to ask for supplies, and to ascertain when and where to be dropped.

D. A. Clay
The Guards Armoured Division was based at Welbeck Abbey Estate.

Proteus Camp at Ollerton on the A614 complete with its own narrow gauge railway and hundreds of Nissen huts full of ammunition of all shapes and sizes.

R.A.F. Cuckney Maintenance and Supply Depot on the Cuckney to Budby Road. Concrete base remains can still be seen in the woods.

Henley Hall being used as a canteen for the forces.

D. Smith.

I remember the crash landing of bi-plane trainer in fields near New England Way the Polish pilot was unhurt. He came from RAF Newton.

I think in 1943 a German fighter pilot crashed and was killed, in 'Big Bend' field by side of a wood next to Pleasley Vale Mills. Also I think in 1944 a German bomber crashed between Stuffynwood Hall and Warsop railway line. He had dumped bombs on Shirebrook which resulted in casualties. Two Germans bailed out and were caught by the Home Guard, the rest were killed in the crash.

USA paratroopers did some of their training at Hardwick Hall.

USA Army hospital. I can remember The American King's Mill patients in wheelchairs being wheeled around the reservoir.

Women's Land Army Hostel was situated just before the Rat Hole going from Clipstone towards Old Clipstone on the right hand side.

The Boughton Ordnance Depot was used by the R.A.F. in wartime.

The old quarry between Fisher Lane and Windsor Road was used by the Home Guard for Blacker Bombard and other weapons target practice.

American soldiers brawling in the Black Boy pub on the Market, the sound of American sirens and several jeeps and a lorry full of 'snowballs' (American military police, so named because of their white helmets, gaiters and webbing) tearing down Stockwell Gate and coming to a halt outside the pub. Snowballs lining up the steps from the back of the lorry. Then some of the biggest entered the pub and American soldiers were thrown out of the pub, through the line of Snowballs, and slung into the back of the lorry. The Snowballs followed them and the little convoy retreated back to the American Camp on Sutton Road

Evacuees
Mrs Fearn
St. John's Church hall was used as registration centre for evacuees.

Entertainment
L. Orton.
I can remember that Proctor's fairground was in Toothill Lane instead of the Market Place as it was partially protected.

Roadblocks
D.A. Clay
On the A60 just over the top of Cuckney Hill, on the left hand side, can be found the remains of another roadblock.

Police
D. A. Clay
My, father, Alfred Clay, was a police war reserve constable. When war was declared he was sent to guard the petrol tanks at the top of Wharf Road. He was then sent to the water tower on Berry Hill Lane. He had to stand on top of the tower in case German paratroopers landed. Other men who were on duty there were Walter Keeton, Frank Lager, Mr Bills and Mr Dawson.

End of war street party for children.

TIMELINE
Tom Gamble

1938
29 Sept. Gas masks distributed at local schools. Trenches dug in Can Bank, Clumber St., Queen St., Bath Lane, Titchfield Park. Underground shelters surveyed in town centre. Warnings of air raids and gas attacks announced. Mayor read royal proclamations from steps of Town Hall calling out some Reservists. Appeal for additional ARP volunteers. Warnings against food hoarding appeared.

14 Oct. Air raid sirens tested.

1939
6 Jan. Mansfield classified a reception area for refugees and evacuees.

20 Jan. Black-out practice announced for 1am - 3am.

27 Jan. The Mayor announces survey of accommodation available for evacuees.

21 Apr. Appeal for volunteers to bring Sherwood Foresters T.A. unit up to war strength.

6 June Air raid sirens tested and found audible throughout town's boundaries.

18 Aug. Local preparations completed for compiling national register and the issue of identity cards

1 Sept. First black-out imposed. Gas masks must now be carried at all times. Caves behind business premises in town centre adapted as shelters.

2 Sept. 80 expectant mothers and 53 small children evacuated from Sheffield arrived at High Oakham School for dispersal to volunteer accommodation.

4 Sept. Shelter for 200 people built on Radmanthwaite Estate by Mr.J.S.Bames. Residents on Intake Estate digging tunnels and filling sandbags to make Shelter for 1000 people. 5 Sept. Pupils from HighPavement and Manning Secondary School assembled at King-Edward, Ravensdale, and Bull Farm Schools to be allocated to Accommodation.

6 Sept. 57-expectant mothers and 45 children from Nottingham assembled at Berry Hill Open Air School to be found accommodation.

7 Oct. 118 pupils from High Pavement directed to (QEGs(Boys) and 50 from Manning Secondary to QEGS(Girls).

1940
5 Jan. Rosemary Senior Mixed School to be closed and taken over by the military.

8 Jan. Householders to register for meat ration.

23 Jan. Mayor opens War Fund to provide parcels and knitted comforts for over 1,000 servicemen.

16 Jan. Canteens for servicemen set up at Henley Hall, St.Peter's, Leeming St. and the Old Meeting House.

24 May. First news published of local servicemen missing or taken prisoner.

31 May. Arrival of civilian refugees from Belgium.

2 June. Arrival of 850 child evacuees from Southend-on-Sea.

14 June. Launch of Savings for Victory Campaign in Mansfield.

22 July. Registration for butter and cooking fat. Tea rationed.

2 Aug. Mayor announces scheme for local councils to buy "Sherwood Forest Spitfire."

14 Aug. Visit by Princess Royal to inspect local ATS units.

29 Nov. War Weapons Week in Mansfield raised £388,955.

1941
10 Jan. Street fire-fighting groups to be trained by Fire Brigade to deal with incendiary bombs.

15 May. Municipal Restaurant opened in the old Picturedrome in Belvedere St.
21 June. First Lord of Admiralty took salute at parade outside County Technical College to open Savings Week (raising £606,774).
1 Aug. Home Guard in mock battle on land South of Mansfield.
23 Aug. Registration for milk rationing.
14 Sept. All males aged 18-60 years must enrol for Civil Defence duties.
24 Oct. Town Clerk announces requisitioning of all unnecessary iron and steel railings in Mansfield.

1942

2 Jan. Start of salvage collection, including waste paper and household waste for pig-swill.
9 Feb. Soap rationing begins.
13 Mar. Warship Week in Mansfield and Mansfield Woodhouse raising £442,031 to adopt HMS destroyer Icarus.
3 July. Newly formed HQ Company of Mansfield Battalion Home Guard in camp at Berry Hill Park.
Dec. "Elizabethan" publishes details of 417 QEGS Old Boys in forces, Numbers of casualties, prisoners and distinctions.

1943

3 Jan. Exchange of plaques at Granada cinema to commemorate adoption of HMS Icarus.
19 Jun. Wings for Victory Week programme includes contributions by USA and Polish forces.
2 July Wings for Victory total £620,040; individual and group results published.

1944

11 Feb. Domestic-coal supplies restricted to 5 cwt. per month.
3 June War Savings Week.

1945

11 Mar. Tribute to work of Civil Defence Services in Mansfield paid by Lord Trent, the Regional Commissioner for Civil Defence.
4 May. Licensed premises and dance halls to have one hour extension on VE Day.
13 May. Victory Sunday marked by church service and parade by ATC. Civic service at parish church attended by 1,100 people. Street parties.
15 Aug. 2,000 people gathered in the early hours in Market Place celebrating end of hostilities following Japan's surrender. Flags, bonfire. Civic gathering outside Town Hall, addressed by the Mayor.